McLAREN M23

1973 onwards (all marks)

© Haynes Publishing 2013

Ian Wagstaff has asserted his right to be identified
as the author of this work.

First published in June 2013

A catalogue record for this book is available
from the British Library

ISBN 978 0 85733 312 4

Library of Congress control no. 2013932254

Published by Haynes Publishing,
Sparkford, Yeovil, Somerset BA22 7JJ, UK
Tel: 01963 442030 Fax: 01963 440001
Int. tel: +44 1963 442030 Int. fax: +44 1963 440001
E-mail: sales@haynes.co.uk
Website: www.haynes.co.uk

Haynes North America Inc.,
861 Lawrence Drive, Newbury Park,
California 91320, USA

Printed in the USA by Odcombe Press LP,
1299 Bridgestone Parkway, La Vergne, TN 37086

COVER CUTAWAY: *Tony Matthews*

McLAREN M23

1973 onwards (all marks)

Owners' Workshop Manual

An insight into the design, engineering, maintenance and operation of McLaren's legendary Formula 1 car

Ian Wagstaff

Contents

Introduction

In carrying out research for this book, I came across my lap chart for the 1975 British Grand Prix. I prided myself on my ability to keep lap charts, but this one had been completely 'blown'. By lap 21 I am obviously having trouble with my pen, and have only noted the first nine runners. Four laps later I can only record the leader, and the word 'rain' is scrawled upon the page. I slightly recover to be able to record the first five or six runners for a while, but after lap 48 there is nothing except the legend 'stopped at 56 laps'. At some later date, and in the dry, I have recorded the result: 1st number one, the reigning World Champion, Emerson Fittipaldi, in his McLaren M23. It was to be his last Grand Prix victory.

Perhaps unfairly, I tend to associate significant moments in the life of the M23 with rain. Two years later, James Hunt, like Fittipaldi in 1974, took the World Championship with an M23, a year-long contest that finished in the downpour at

Fuji. The car's final podium at a major Formula 1 race came in the *Daily Express* International Trophy at Silverstone in 1978. The conditions were appalling; I was running the press office at Silverstone that day and wondering why on earth I had been so keen to work at the place.

Finally, we come to Donington Park, many decades later and the film set of *Rush!* It is a warm day and most of us are standing around in shirtsleeves. However, the 'marshals' are clad in orange wet-weather ponchos, and as the cars, including two M23s (one of them driven by Jochen Mass), blast off the grid down towards Redgate, so the overhead rain machines drench the track. This is not Donington 2012, it is Fuji 1976… and it is raining again.

There were, of course, many days during the career of the McLaren M23 when the sun really shone. By the end of 1976 it had become one of the truly great Grand Prix cars, as the following pages will, I hope, indicate.

Acknowledgements

Those who worked for McLaren in its original guises were a tight-knit bunch, many of whom remain in touch with each other. The assistance of a number of them has been invaluable, and the time spent in their company has been most enjoyable. Not only did they give up their time to reminisce, but some of them also took the trouble to read relevant parts of the manuscript. My gratitude goes to Kerry Adams, Gary Anderson, Alastair Caldwell, Gordon Coppuck, Tony Griffiths, Robin Herd, John Hornby, David Luff, John Nicholson, Roy Reader, Mark Scott and Leo Wybrott. From the current staff of Nicholson McLaren I must also add John Waghorn and Tony Ireland.

It is also intriguing to hear what the drivers of the time now think of the M23, so my thanks to Emerson Fittipaldi, David Hobbs, John McCormack, Jochen Mass, Jody Scheckter and Tony Trimmer. Interviewing a race-suited Jochen on the set of *Rush!* at Donington next to a full grid of 1976 Grand Prix cars has to have been surreal.

From the ranks of past and current M23 owners and those who prepare the cars, my gratitude goes to John Anderson, Steve Earle, Joaquin Folch-Rusiñol, Greg Galdi, Richard Meins, Scott Walker, Adam Brock (Mandarin Motorsport), Matt Byrne, Ian Cox, Chris Davies and Jonathan Hoad (WDK Motorsport), Rick and Rob Hall (Hall and Hall) and Bob Simpson (R&J Simpson Engineering).

Others to thank include Nigel Beresford, Gordon Bruce, Glenda Gephart, Jim Hajicosta, Adrian Hamilton, Robin Harman, Stuart McCrudden, Jan McLaren, Marcus Pye, John Surtees and Jennifer Revson. My apologies to those I may have inadvertently missed.

All photos are credited, but again this book would not be what it is without the assistance of Dave Hill, archive librarian at Ford Photographic. Jeff Bloxham came up with obscure photos of M23s even on a Sunday afternoon, while my thanks also go to Zoe Schafer at LAT and, once again, David Luff who managed to combine the roles of mechanic and photographer at CarFest 2012. Nicky Aigner and Jon Bunston are to be thanked for their photos from the making of *Rush!*, as are Stewart Clark, Mark Coughlin, Wayne Ellwood, Curtis Jacobson, Andrew Noakes, Nicholas Phoenix and Mark Windecker, for their contributions

Amongst the authors of secondary sources consulted, two stand out. That consummate historian Doug Nye is one, and the other is my all-time motorsport hero, the late Denis Jenkinson. It was 'Jenks' who painstakingly recorded the identities of the M23s at every Grand Prix and, even if Alastair Caldwell questions their complete accuracy, because of the way that chassis plates could be swapped, this is the nearest we will ever come to a complete picture.

Once again, I must acknowledge the assistance given by leading motor racing engineer Andy Brown. Finally, as he had done for the Lotus 72 owners' manual, Steve Rendle of Haynes Publishing has proved to be the ideal editor.

Ian Wagstaff   January 2013

'The basic principle of the M16 with a Cosworth DFV engine would be a much lighter package than the M19, so we thought, let's make it like that.'

Gordon Coppuck
McLaren M23 designer

(Ford)

Chapter One

The McLaren M23 story

━━━━━━●━━━━━━

When Gordon Coppuck designed the McLaren M23, he created one of the supreme cars of the 3-litre Grand Prix era. It was a straightforward design that successfully competed in top-line Formula 1 races for six years, taking McLaren to its first Constructors' Championship as well as to two World Drivers' titles, the second of these being won in the most dramatic style.

The earliest known ancestor of the McLaren M23 might be said to be a 1929 Ulster Austin Seven that frightened New Zealand garage proprietor, Les McLaren. After a first drive, McLaren was all for disposing of the uncontrollable little car, but his son Bruce managed to persuade him otherwise. It was to be the stuff of legend, as the 14-year-old Bruce, whose childhood had been blighted by a diseased hip, took over maintenance of the car and, when old enough, went racing with it.

Bruce quickly rose to the top in his country's motor sport, winning the New Zealand International Grand Prix Association's 'Driver-to-Europe' scholarship. In 1958, he travelled to England where it had been arranged for him to race a Formula 2 Cooper. Within a year he was a Cooper Formula 1 factory driver and, in December 1959, he became the youngest driver to win a World Championship Grand Prix when he came first at Sebring. The following season, McLaren finished second in the World Championship behind his team leader Jack Brabham.

Brabham left Cooper to build his own cars, leaving McLaren to inherit the team's number one spot. Cooper had, though, seen its best days and, in 1966, McLaren followed his fellow Antipodean by becoming a Formula 1 constructor. However, it was during his last year with Cooper that cars began to appear with the McLaren name; and it was sports cars that first established the brand. Having purchased and rebuilt Roger Penske's Cooper-based Zerex Special sports racer with a McLaren-designed tube frame, Bruce became very much involved in the Group 7 scene, the massive V8-powered sports cars; the quickest things around in the 1960s. The first car constructed under the McLaren name was the Oldsmobile-powered M1A of 1964. Production versions were made available, manufactured at Elva Cars. A succession of massively successful Group 7 cars followed, although now Chevrolet-powered. Such became the level of dominance of this type of racing that the North America-based Can-Am Challenge became known as the 'Bruce and Denny Show' after McLaren and teammate Denny Hulme. McLaren factory drivers took the championship for five consecutive years from 1967 to 1971.

ABOVE: The founder, Bruce McLaren.
(Author)

RIGHT: The car that began it all, the 750cc Austin that McLaren first hillclimbed at Muriwai Beach, setting fastest time in his class. 'Pop' McLaren stands behind his son.
(Bruce McLaren Trust, www.bruce-mclaren.com)

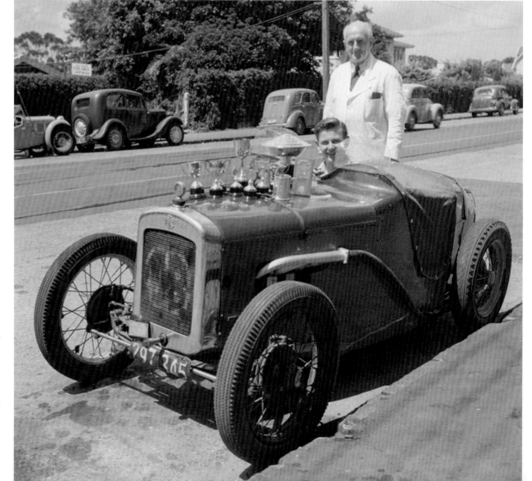

Foray into Formula 1

For his foray into Formula 1 construction, McLaren hired as designer Robin Herd, a young aerospace engineer with a double first at Oxford. Herd, who was later to become one of the founders of March, was told that the McLaren team was about to set off for the Tasman Series in Australia and New Zealand (where it would be racing Coopers) and would be away for four months. Would he like to design its first Formula 1 car and begin the build while the team was away? 'I had never worked on cars but I knew about them,' recalled Herd.

Thanks to the use of Mallite, a composite laminate of special 26-gauge aluminium sheets bonded over an eighth-inch sandwich filling of end-grain balsawood, Herd's M2B was one of the stiffest open-cockpit racers built. McLaren reckoned the M2B was 'phenomenal' to drive. Herd put that down to its rigidity. After the flexible Coopers that he had been driving, it was a feature the New Zealander could not help but appreciate. Engine choice, though, proved the

downfall of the car. Neither a heavy, linered-down Ford V8 Indy engine nor a Serenissima V8 was up to the job, although the latter powered McLaren to sixth place and the marque's first World Championship point at the British Grand Prix.

When reminded that the M2B 'won' the World Championship, Herd grins and observes whimsically, 'I don't like to boast.' The M2B fictionally took the title as the car that stood in for the 'Yamura' driven by 'Pete Aron' in

ABOVE: Bruce was at the wheel for the marque's first Grand Prix win, the 1968 race at Spa. Only Jack Brabham had ever won such a race in a car bearing his own name. *(LAT)*

BELOW: A one-off appearance: Derek Bell drove the heavy four-wheel-drive M9A at Silverstone in 1969. Cosworth, Lotus and Matra also found such systems wanting that year. *(Author)*

the 1966 John Frankenheimer film, *Grand Prix*. Nearly half a century later, another McLaren would star in another feature film, *Rush!*, only this time it would be as itself and the story would be based on reality, although no less dramatic. That car was the McLaren M23.

McLaren commenced the 1967 season with a stop-gap, undersized 2.1-litre V8 BRM-engined Formula 2 car, the M4B, before Herd's next design, the M5A (with its full 3-litre V12 BRM engine) was ready. The engine that was to dominate the years to come, the V8 Cosworth DFV, appeared that season powering Team Lotus cars. Herd, assisted by Gordon Coppuck, who was to become the father of the M23, designed a simple car, the M7A, to take the Ford-backed engine for 1968, the year that Bruce McLaren Motor Racing really established itself as a front-rank Grand Prix

team. Bruce took the marque's first Grand Prix win in Belgium, Hulme followed up by finishing first in Italy and Canada, and the team was awarded second place in the Constructors' Championship. The M7A continued for a second season, with Hulme taking the Mexican Grand Prix, while a four-wheel-drive car, the M9A, appeared briefly at the British Grand Prix, driven by Derek Bell, before going the way of all 1969 four-wheel-drive F1 cars. The M14A and M14D, which was based on a simplified version of Coppuck's M7C, were introduced for 1970, with Gordon involved in the detailing.

The date 2 June 1970 should have been just a conventional test day at Goodwood, the Sussex track. The McLaren team had recently received a setback when Hulme's hands had been badly burned at Indianapolis. McLaren, checking out a new Can-Am M8D, had accelerated hard out of the Lavant Corner and was on the straight heading for Woodcote when the huge tail body section was ripped off the car because of the absence of a securing pin. The car hurtled into the bank protecting an old marshal's post and McLaren was killed instantly.

The New Zealander had created a resolute team that, while devastated, pulled together inspired by Hulme who, although now emotionally as well as physically hurt, was quickly back in the cockpit. Dan Gurney stepped in to assist and Peter Gethin also

ABOVE: According to
Gordon Coppuck, the
twin inspirations for
the M23 were the side-
radiatored M16 Indy
car and... (Indianapolis
Motor Speedway)

LEFT: ...the Cosworth-
DFV-powered M19.
(Ford)

joined the team. Within less than a fortnight, Gurney honoured Bruce's name in the best way by winning the next round of the Can-Am series.

It would, however, be 1972 before a McLaren car again won a Grand Prix. In addition to DFVs, V8 Alfa Romeo engines were also tried in M7D and M14D cars, but it was not until the advent of the attractive DFV-engined M19, designed by Ralph Bellamy, that the team again took the chequered flag first in a Grand Prix, with Hulme victorious in South Africa. As well as Formula 1, McLaren had by this time established itself as a highly successful manufacturer over a number of formulae. Can-Am continued to be dominated for a while after Bruce's death with American Peter Revson, who was to partner Hulme in the Formula 1 team the following season, becoming champion in 1971. In addition, McLaren's M10A and M10B had been the class of the field in Formula 5000, while the 1972 and 1974 Indianapolis 500 races were to fall to its chisel-shaped M16s. In Formula 2, a young South African called Jody Scheckter was indicating his potential with the immaculate factory-entered M21.

First season for the M23

A change in the Formula 1 regulations, mandating fuel tanks to be protected by deformable structures, gave McLaren the opportunity to replace the worthy, but perhaps unspectacular, M19 for 1973. The new Gordon Coppuck-designed car, the M23, is of course the subject of detailed examination in this book, but suffice it to say at this point that it was visually as different from the M19 as the Lotus 72 had been from the Lotus 49 three years earlier.

The first test for the prototype chassis M23/1 took place at Goodwood, where the car was attended by Denny Hulme's mechanic Kevin Stone and two of project manager Leo Wybrott's build team. It ran well and trouble free; Hulme was impressed. It was then shipped to South Africa for the third Grand Prix of the season. Despite his years in Formula 1 and the fact that he had won the World Championship with Brabham in 1967, Denny had never before sat on the pole for a Grand Prix. That changed on 3 March 1973, for Hulme had set fastest time earlier in the week with the new car, and he then protected his pole position the day before the race despite a leaking radiator. McLaren also had two M19s in the race, and

to make matters even better for the team, local man Jody Scheckter, in his second Grand Prix, had been third fastest and was occupying the outside of the front row of the grid. For the first two laps Hulme ran away with the race, but the fairytale beginning did not last long.

On the third lap a number of drivers were involved in an accident that left Clay Regazzoni trapped in a burning BRM. The Swiss driver was saved thanks to the heroism of Mike Hailwood, who subsequently received the George Medal for his bravery, and a marshal who pulled him clear. The name of Hailwood

ABOVE: A Yardley publicity photo for the launch of the M23. *(David Luff collection)*

RIGHT: Denny Hulme and Teddy Mayer at the M23's unveiling. *(LAT)*

LEFT: The first time the M23 was seen in anger in Britain was at the Brands Hatch Race of Champions in 1973. (Author)

will shortly return to this story. For the M23, the accident meant an end to a stunning debut. Debris from the incident punctured one of Hulme's tyres. He pitted for a replacement. Four laps later he was back in the pits for another, but he recovered from being way back in 19th place to finish fifth.

It was a while before the M23 performed quite as well again, with only a few minor placings in the next three Grands Prix for Hulme and Revson, who had also now moved up from the M19. Even the early season, non-championship races at Brands Hatch and Silverstone could only yield a second and a fourth for Hulme and Revson respectively. Then came the Swedish Grand Prix at Anderstorp. Practice did not indicate anything special; Hulme was sixth, Revson seventh. It seemed to get worse. Early in the race, Denny was baulked by Jackie Oliver's Shadow, and dirt was thrown

into his throttle slides. He lost time before these cleared, and by now 'the Bear' was in a bad mood. With rev-limiter switched off, he charged up to second, and when, with two laps to go, a tyre on Ronnie Peterson's Lotus punctured, he swept into the lead. The McLaren M23 had taken its first victory.

ABOVE: The initial victory for the M23 went to Hulme in the 1973 Swedish Grand Prix. (Ford)

THE NEWS 'LEAK'

Gordon Coppuck recalled Jacky Ickx's one-off M23 drive: 'Leo Wybrott (then acting as chief mechanic on the Yardley car) said, "Wouldn't it be great if Jacky Ickx [who had been released by Ferrari] drove one of our cars." He then phoned Autosport to say that Jacky was going to drive the McLaren at the Nürburgring. Jacky received that week's Autosport in Belgium and saw, to his surprise, that he was racing for McLaren at the 'Ring. So, he drove to the track and got there the same time as us. With Leo pressuring, Jacky got to have the spare car. Well, he was spectacular. We had Peter and Denny as our normal drivers, and he was quicker than them. Talk about upset! Normally, we were a pretty smooth-running

team, but Peter and Denny were absolutely furious. It was decided that we would knock at least 500 revs off Jacky's engine, put him on the hardest tyres in the race, and he was not to embarrass our boys any more. He still came third. You can't imagine that as a modern scenario!'

ABOVE: Gordon Coppuck said that Jacky Ickx was as surprised as anyone to read in Autosport that he would be racing an M23 at the Nürburgring. (Ford)

ABOVE: The first occasion that Jody Scheckter raced an M23 (Paul Ricard in 1973), he led from the start before tangling with Emerson Fittipaldi. *(Ford)*

BELOW: Revson, heading for his second and final Grand Prix win. 'Our crew was really the key,' he wrote. 'They made the right decision, pitting me as soon as possible and getting me back out on the race track.' *(Ford)*

RIGHT: Teddy Mayer's race report from the 1973 Canadian Grand Prix.

A repeat looked on the cards at Paul Ricard, as Scheckter, standing in for Revson who was competing in the Pocono 500 in the USA, led for 41 laps. The next time round, the vastly more experienced Emerson Fittipaldi tried to take the lead. The South African held his ground and the front wheel of the Lotus hit the McLaren amidships. Fittipaldi, now out of the race, was not amused; Scheckter retired to the pits with damaged suspension.

Come the next round of the championship at Silverstone, Scheckter was back in the news for all the wrong reasons. The story of how he crashed near the front of the field the first time round at Woodcote corner, causing the race to be red flagged and putting nine cars out of the contest, is the stuff of M23 legend. Revson, however, retrieved the day for McLaren. Taking the lead on the 39th lap, he maintained his position for his first Grand Prix win and the M23's second. Hulme was third.

Following a fourth place in Holland, Revson was surprised to find that Ickx had temporarily joined McLaren for the German Grand Prix. The rapid Belgian impressed the team with a third place, despite not having the best equipment that it could offer. The American was back for a third place at Monza. Meanwhile, Hulme seemed to be going through a series of varied problems – broken engine, handling difficulties, an errant plug lead; it all seemed to be happening to him during the second half of the season.

In Canada it rained, it certainly rained. Much diving into the pits to change tyres caused confusion amongst the official lap charters. Pace cars may be commonplace now but in 1973 they were a novelty, and when Scheckter again made himself unpopular by colliding with François Cevert's Tyrrell, one was deployed. This would have been all well and good if the officials had actually known who was leading. As it was, the pace car took station ahead of former McLaren mechanic, Howden Ganley in a Williams. Front runners Jackie Stewart (Tyrrell) and Emerson Fittipaldi (Lotus) were stuck behind the New Zealander, while others, including Revson and Jackie Oliver, who were ahead of Ganley on the road, kept going apace until they had caught up the tail of the pace car-led trail. Following the restart it was generally felt that Oliver was leading, but Fittipaldi was in a determined mood and caught him on what was thought to be the penultimate lap. There was jubilation in the Lotus pit as the Brazilian crossed the line for what they thought was the last time... but no chequered flag. That came down on a close group comprising Ganley, James Hunt (March), Revson and Hailwood (Surtees). Revson was declared the winner, it being said that he had passed Oliver on lap 47 when the latter was experiencing difficulty with sticking throttle slides. It would be three hours before the result could be confirmed. It was hardly the most satisfactory of results, but Revson and the M23 had won again.

The final championship round of the year, the US Grand Prix, saw Hulme and Revson in fourth and fifth places respectively. Revson, though, had long known that he was on his way out. Marlboro sponsorship money was bringing Emerson Fittipaldi to the team. It was hardly an amicable parting. Revson's sister Jennifer remembers, 'Peter was very unhappy, and

FROM: TEAM YARDLEY McLAREN

RACE REPORT   CANADIAN GRAND PRIX   SEPT. 23, 1973

Result: 1st. - Peter Revson   Yardley McLaren
               2nd. - Emerson Fittipaldi   JPS Special
               3rd. - Jackie Oliver   UOP Shadow

My prediction made in the pouring rain ten minutes before the
start of the Canadian Grand Prix that the result could only be a wipe-out
or a disaster was accurate in so far as the McLaren Team was concerned for
most of the weekend and most of the race, but was miraculously knocked on
the head when Revson was given the chequered flag.

Practice started badly for Denny Hulme when a small piece of the
pinion bearing cage broke off, ruined the bearing and seized the entire
gearbox. Luckily the gearbox casing was not damaged and we were able to
repair it, but Denny missed the entire first practice session and only got
one clear lap in the second session.   Meanwhile Revson and Scheckter were
both going well and established second and third fastest times respectively.
As usual Goodyear had three compounds from which to chose, creating a situation
which puts the onus on the team manager to sort out which tyre will be most
raceworthy. I think Ed Alexander from Goodyear actually enjoys watching us
spin our wheels trying to decide which tyre is best.

The first practice session of the second day was a rain out and
none of the McLaren cars bothered to go swimming. Half way through the second
session the track dried out and everyone made a furious effort to improve
his grid position. Revson and Scheckter managed to stay in second and third
spots and Denny moved forward from his lowly twelfth to seventh, despite a
spate of minor problems.

Race morning was another down pour and nobody was looking forward to
sloshing about for 200 miles on Mosport's narrow, bumpy, slippery surface.
During the morning warm-up session six cars crashed and Denny spun and touched
the guard rail, fortunately without damage.   Revson reckoned it was like
driving on a skating rink without skates!

Shortly before the race started a fresh sky-burst left us in absolutely
no doubt as to which tyres we had to start on. Again Goodyear had three wet tyre
compounds but no one knew too much about them because sorting out a wet tyre
is extremely difficult. Track conditions change so rapidly while it rains
that it is almost impossible to tell whether the tyre is better or the track
has improved. Anyway we decided to put Peter, Denny and Jody all on a
different compound in order to cover our bets.   This plan went down the

---

Canadian Grand Prix Report

drain when Revson punctured one of his on the warm-up lap and we had
to put him on to the same tyres as Denny was using.

When the race started Jody moved immediately into second place
behind Peterson, and Revson, using what turned out to be the worse of the
three compounds in the wet, slipped rapidly down the grid. Denny meanwhile
trailed slowly round at the back, indicating severe instability, which
turned out to be a puncture when he pitted on the fifth lap.

After about ten laps, Scheckter passed Peterson, but meantime they
had both been passed by Nicki Lauda in a BRM. Then as the track dried, the
particular compound Jody was using deteriorated and Revson began to move up
a little.

It may well have been lucky that Revson was not competitive
while the track was wet because this almost certainly led to his
decision to make an early pit stop to change to dry tyres. Had he been
on a better wet compound and in a leading position, he might well have
stayed out longer and been in a different position relative to the pace
car. His pit stop on Lap 23 including the time lost coming in and going
out cost him only a minute on the road and this turned out to be probably the
fastest pit stop of the day.

Most cars came in and changed tyres about Lap 30 and since many,
including Emerson reconnected their roll bars and reset their shock absorbers
as well, almost all of those stops were considerably slower than Revson's.

Shortly after changing to dry tyres, Jody and Francois Cevert had
a coming together which resulted in both cars being put out the race badly
damaged, but fortunately with no injury to either driver. Needless to say,
both drivers were very up-set! This crash covered the track with debris
and left Francois' car in a dangerous position so the pace car was put out
in front of Howden Ganley who the race organisers claimed was the leader, but
who was in fact a lap down. The net result was that Fittipaldi was slowed
by the pace car almost immediately, whereas Revson, who was in front of
Ganley on the road, came round and made up most of a lap on Fittipaldi.
This was the deciding factor and led to Revson's winning the race.

Certainly the Yardley McLaren Team had a bit of luck but we felt
a certain amount of luck was overdue after Denny's spate of punctures in
South Africa, Barcelona and France.

                                                    E. E. MAYER.

---

disheartened, with the way Teddy [Mayer] often
treated him, not just at this point but when the
Marlboro sponsorship came along, and Teddy's
best offer to Peter was to demote him to the
second car. Given his recent wins for McLaren,
this was not only a slap in the face but the last
straw for Peter. It was with a heavy heart that
he left McLaren.'

Three's a crowd

The Marlboro cash brought problems for
McLaren. The M23, and the M19 before it,
had appeared in the white, papaya and brown
livery of toiletries-manufacturer Yardley. The
cigarette company's deal was far more lucrative,
but McLaren had a contract with Yardley. Teddy
Mayer had effectively taken over the running of
McLaren following Bruce's death. Lawyer Mayer,
who had first joined the company with his
brother Timmy (who had been killed driving a

Bruce McLaren-entered Cooper in the Tasman
Series), was faced with a quandary, which he
overcame by dividing the Formula 1 operation
into two teams. Fittipaldi and Hulme would drive
for one in the distinctive red and white livery of

**BELOW: A separate
Yardley team was
formed for 1974 with,
initially, Mike Hailwood
driving.** (Ford)

YARDLEY McLAREN
formula 1 briefing

BELGIAN GRAND PRIX
20 May 1973

Editor : Martin Cartwright
Yardley, 33 Old Bond Street, London W1X 4AP Tel : 01-629 9341
Compiled by Alan Brinton
Printed and produced by R.S. Associates, London W.1.

TOUCH AND GO

After overcoming a whole series of problems the Royal Automobile Club de Belgique has finally managed to lay on the fifth round of this year's F1 world championship at Zolder on May 20.

But even up till a few days ago there was considerable doubt whether the Belgian Grand Prix could take place. The major hurdle was the condition of the circuit, which has never before staged a Formula 1 event and which earlier this year did not match up to the requirements laid down by the CSI. A heavy programme of improvements was called for and then, when these were almost completed, it was discovered that the resurfacing of the 2.6 miles circuit was unsatisfactory, and it had to be done again. That it was done is a tribute to the enthusiasm and energy of those responsible, but surely there has never been a motor racing pre-GP cliff-hanger like this.

For all the teams Zolder is a new challenge, for though a number of the drivers have raced there previously — Denny Hulme won a Formula 2 event there in 1964 — it now has a slowing-down chicane-type tweak before the notorious hump on the back stretch behind the pits. In addition, the resurfacing is an unknown factor, and the two competing tyre firms go to this Grand Prix armed with more than the usual number of different tyres since they simply do not know what is going to work best. Since circuit work was due to continue right up to the last minute, it was thought virtually certain that there would be no opportunity for any teams to carry out any testing prior to official practice.

Another problem is the sand surrounding the course which is bound to blow across the surface, or be kicked on to the track by cars putting a wheel off the shoulder.

The line-up of cars and drivers for this fifth round in the 1973 world championship — which also carries the courtesy title of Grand Prix of Europe — will be virtually identical to that seen recently at Barcelona. There is a possibility, though, of the Tecno finally making its debut with Chris Amon at the wheel, while Rikki von Opel was hoping to debut his new Ensign providing testing went satisfactorily a few days earlier. It also looks as though Claude Bouroigne will be getting his first chance in Formula 1, driving a Surtees.

Because the circuit is such an unknown factor — only Emerson Fittipaldi has been there with a Grand Prix car, and the track has been resurfaced again since he was there — it is more than usually difficult to make any assessment of chances, though current form would suggest three teams to make the running — John Player Team Lotus, Yardley McLaren and Elf-Tyrrell.

After his great exploits at Barcelona, where a seized gearbox robbed him of what had looked like being his first Grand Prix victory, Ronnie Peterson must surely be reckoned with in his John Player Special. If, as Denny Hulme says, Zolder has many of the characteristics of the Brands Hatch short circuit, then it should suit the dashing technique of Ronnie very well.

Emerson's nearest rival in the championship table is Jackie Stewart, whose run at Barcelona was cut short by brake failure on his Tyrell-Ford, but who has demonstrated that he is on top form. So too is his French teammate, Francois Cevert, whose second place at Barcelona brought him into third place in the championship battle.

So far this season victory has eluded the Yardley McLaren pair — Denny Hulme and Peter Revson. There can be no doubt that the Gordon Coppuck-designed McLaren M23 is a strong contender for top honours, and but for niggling problems in Barcelona both Yardley McLaren drivers would have been higher placed.

There is something about racing in front of a home crowd that adds zest to the attitude of any driver, and Jacky Ickx must be determined to show his fellow Belgians that he and his new Ferrari are a winning combination. Jacky was very satisfied with the first outing of the Ferrari at Barcelona, and if it has been possible to sort out the reaiability then he must be reckoned a top challenger.

The Surtees duo of Hailwood and Pace have had miserable luck so far this season, and surely deserve better. The same could be said of the Brabham equipe with Carlos Reutemann still chasing the points in the BT42 which so nearly won in Spain.

Somehow, too, one always expects the Marlboro BRM team to turn up trumps, particularly with Clay Regazzoni returning to good form after his South African near-disaster, but unless they can avoid a repeat of their tyre problems at Montjuich they must be ruled out.

There can always be a surprise result in any Grand Prix — as witness the Beltoise victory at Monaco last year in the rain — but if anyone is looking for drivers to back in this Belgian race, the list of possibles would appear to contain seven names — Fittipaldi, Stewart, Cevert, Hulme, Revson, Ickx and Peterson. And not necessarily in that order. If Emerson would give someone else a chance it would make the world championship battle much more interesting !

TIMETABLE
PRACTICE:

FRIDAY, MAY 18

Formula 1	17.00—19.00

SATURDAY, MAY 19

Formula Super Vee	11.00—12.00
Formula 1	14.00—15.00
Formula Super Vee	15.30—16.30
Formula 1	17.00—18.00

RACES:
SUNDAY, MAY 20

Formula Super Vee (20 laps)	13.30
Belgian Grand Prix (70 laps)	15.30

Next world championship round: Monaco Grand Prix, June '3

Marlboro, while the brave Mike Hailwood joined to race a third M23, which would be run by Phil Kerr as part of a separately run operation. Backing for the red and white cars would also come from lubricant supplier Texaco.

Fittipaldi, World Champion in 1972 with Lotus, immediately proved his worth as an enthusiastic tester. However, it was Hulme who scored first in Argentina with what was to be his final Grand Prix victory. Fittipaldi inadvertently knocked off his ignition, a fact that he can now look back on with a wry smile. He made up for his mistake two weeks later, winning in his native Brazil having battled with Lotus's Ronnie Peterson in the opening laps.

It was a competitive year. Hailwood scored his best place of the season with a third in South Africa. Tragically, former M23 driver Peter Revson had been killed at the Kyalami track during pre-race testing a few days before driving for his new team, Shadow. It was Fittipaldi's turn to come third in Spain, and then time for another victory for the Brazilian in the Belgian Grand Prix at Nivelles. It was the second year that the race had been held there, the daunting Spa-Francorchamps circuit now being deemed too dangerous for Grand Prix racing. Fittipaldi took the lead when Ferrari driver Clay Regazzoni – benefiting from a dubious pole position lap time – took to the grass overtaking a backmarker, grimly holding it for the rest of the race as he battled with Regazzoni's teammate Niki Lauda. Team manager Alastair Caldwell recalled how wing angle had been taken off Fittipaldi's car that morning to make him faster on the straights and how he was then able to fend off the otherwise quicker Ferraris which were 'all over him' on the bends. 'Emerson never missed a gear, never ran wide, and they just had to sit behind him.' The M23 was now, undoubtedly, a serial Grand Prix winner.

For the next three races, Fittipaldi managed point-scoring placings. The championship that year was divided into two parts, with the best scores from each part added together at the end of the season. The first part was now at an end, and the Brazilian headed the table with 31 points, just three ahead of Regazzoni. Hailwood and Hulme had not fared so well, but were in fifth and joint-sixth places with 11 and 10 points respectively. The second sector

of the year started badly in France, with just one point for Hulme's sixth place. However, at Brands Hatch, Fittipaldi returned to the top of the championship table by finishing second to former M23 driver Jody Scheckter, who was now with Tyrrell.

Not one McLaren finished the German Grand Prix. The event was particularly disastrous for the Yardley-backed team. There were now two cars at Hailwood's disposal, but the former motorcycle world champion crashed the earlier of these in practice following front suspension failure. At the start, Fittipaldi struggled to get into first gear, there was a clash of wheels with teammate Hulme that led to the New Zealander's immediate retirement and the Brazilian's on lap three. By lap 13, Hailwood was battling for fourth place when his M23 landed awkwardly at Pflanzgarten. The car veered to the right and hit the guard rail. This time Hailwood was not able to walk away from the crash, having sustained serious leg injuries that would bring an end to a feisty four-wheel career. The nine times motorcycle world champion did, though, return to two wheels in 1978 and 1979, adding to his eventual total of 14 Isle of Man Tourist Trophy wins. For the final races of the season, David Hobbs and then up-and-coming German Jochen Mass took over as the Yardley team's driver. For Mass it was to be the beginning of a long relationship with the M23.

Hulme came second in Austria, but with two DNFs (did not finish) Fittipaldi had fallen

OPPOSITE: Yardley was an enthusiastic sponsor that reckoned its sales of men's toiletries rose by 17% thanks to motor sport. (David Luff collection)

ABOVE: Yardley McLaren stickers abounded in the early 1970s. Mike Hailwood signed this one for journalist-to-be Marcus Pye.

BELOW: Fittipaldi in Canada, 1974. The Brazilian took the pole and went on to receive the chequered flag. (Ford)

behind Regazzoni in the World Championship stakes. Matters improved when Fittipaldi chased Peterson hard in the Italian Grand Prix, finishing less than a second behind. The Italian tifosi were stunned when Regazzoni retired with engine failure; the initiative had passed back from Ferrari to McLaren, although Regazzoni still headed the table, a point ahead of a latterly consistent Scheckter and three ahead of Fittipaldi. Lauda was also still in the reckoning. It got even better for McLaren in Canada. There, Fittipaldi claimed pole position, going on to win once pacesetter Lauda had crashed on the debris from John Watson's Brabham.

And so it was like this: Fittipaldi had 52 points, Regazzoni had 52 points and, should the pair of them falter, Scheckter was still in there with 45. The teams travelled straight to Watkins Glen for the final and deciding race of the season, coincidentally also the 250th World Championship round since Giuseppe Farina had won the inaugural race at Silverstone in his Alfa Romeo 158 back in 1950. Regazzoni had crashed in a pre-race test session, but a new Ferrari had been flown out from Italy and he seemed to be suffering from little other than a bruised leg. Practice did not go well for the title contenders. Fittipaldi had brake problems, while both Regazzoni and Scheckter had blown

engines. By the Sunday morning Fittipaldi was back on the grid in eighth, Regazzoni was ninth, and Scheckter was not that far ahead of them in sixth.

By the end of the first lap, Scheckter, Fittipaldi and Regazzoni were fifth, sixth and seventh respectively. However, the Swiss driver was finding the handling of his Ferrari so unpredictable that he was falling back. Pit stops for new tyres and then to have the front suspension adjusted put him right out of contention. All Fittipaldi had to do was keep going. Meanwhile, Hulme's DFV engine had blown, bringing an unspectacular end to a significant career. A few days later he would announce his retirement. On lap 45, Scheckter suffered a broken fuel pipe and the World Championship was virtually Fittipaldi's again. With Regazzoni way back in 11th, fourth place was sufficient to take the title. The Brazilian and Swiss had both scored 24 points in the second sector of the season, leaving the former three points ahead. Significantly, McLaren had also taken its first Constructors' title with 73 points. It would be another decade before it won its next, thus making it the only one of the pre-McLaren International era. (The Formula 1 Constructors' Championship had been added to the Drivers' contest in 1958 when it had been won by another British constructor, Vanwall.)

The year in between

The 1975 season began well for the new World Champion with a clever tactical win in Argentina after James Hunt (Hesketh) had spun, followed by second place in Brazil. With the Yardley team now a thing of the past, Jochen Mass had moved up to the Marlboro squad and finished third at Interlagos. The omens looked good, but it was not to continue. The team came away from South Africa with just one point. True, it then won the Spanish Grand Prix, but in tragic circumstances, and Mass was awarded just 4.5 points for what was to be the only Grand Prix win of his career. The Armco barriers at Montjuich Park had not been properly installed, and for a while during practice most of the drivers refused to go out. Team personnel were seen tightening up the guard rails themselves before reminders about contractual obligations forced the competitors on to the track. Fittipaldi did the bare minimum of laps, qualified in last place and then withdrew as a protest.

An accident-strewn race took place, with around half the field being eliminated before one-third distance had been run. Then on the 26th lap the rear aerofoil of Rolf Stommelen's Hill broke away, pitching the car into the guard rails and then into Carlos Pace's Brabham before mounting the top rail, demolishing spectator fencing and killing four bystanders. The race continued for another four laps, which delayed rescue operations, and during this time Mass overtook Jacky Ickx's Lotus for the lead. Because the race was stopped before 60% of the schedule distance, the six top finishers were only awarded half the normal number of points. (In sixth place was the March of Lella Lombardi, the only time to date that a lady has scored points in a World Championship race, albeit a scant 0.5.)

Fittipaldi finished second in Monaco, with no scores in Belgium and Sweden, leaving him in third place at the halfway point of the championship. Again he failed to score in Holland. Some queried his commitment, but then came the British Grand Prix. During the early part of the race he appeared to be content to sit back, but with the rain starting to fall on about lap 20 he moved forward to challenge

the Brabham of Carlos Pace. Several pitted for wet tyres, but Fittipaldi remained out, coping with the slippery conditions and taking the lead. Improved conditions sent those on wets scurrying back to the pits to change again, but then came a cloudburst of such proportions that 16 drivers crashed as a consequence. Fittipaldi did pit this time, took on wets and then kept it on the track for one more lap, during which time the officials decided that conditions were untenable and hung out the chequered flag. It was to be Emerson's final Grand Prix victory, although he was again to show his mettle at Monza where he drove a feisty race to split the Ferraris. In Watkins Glen he came second again after having been shamelessly blocked by the lapped Regazzoni who was helping his teammate, the new World Champion Lauda, to get away. Eventually Regazzoni was shown the black flag, but it was too late for Fittipaldi to do anything about the fleeing Austrian. He had finished the championship in second position but 9.5 points behind the rampant Lauda. Apart from his Spanish Grand Prix win, Mass had three third places to his credit and finished eighth overall. Fittipaldi then dropped a proverbial bombshell, surprising those who had thought he was preparing to retire. He was about to leave McLaren and join his brother Wilson's untried Copersucar team.

ABOVE: **The last Grand Prix win of Fittipaldi's career, the rain-curtailed 1975 British Grand Prix.** *(Ford)*

The dramatic second championship

McLaren was left without a star driver, and James Hunt (who had scored his first Grand Prix victory in 1975) was left without a place following the withdrawal of the Hesketh team. It was a marriage made… well, at least in Colnbrook. It was certainly to lead to one of the most dramatic years in the championship, a year sufficiently full of drama that in 2013 it would become the subject of a feature film, *Rush!*.

Gordon Coppuck's latest design, the M26, was on its way, but the trusty M23 would have to remain the mainstay of the team for some while yet. As will be explained later, the M23 was becoming a different animal with its innovative six-speed gearbox and a new appearance from the Spanish Grand Prix onwards, thanks to a much lower airbox.

Hunt started the season well, with his first ever Grand Prix pole at Interlagos. However, a dislodged injection trumpet led to a throttle jamming open and a spin into the catch fencing. Ominously, the reigning champion Lauda won again in his Ferrari. Hunt took the pole again in South Africa, and this time he came second to the Austrian following a conservative start to preserve his clutch. With Lauda's tyre beginning slowly to deflate, it had been a gripping last few laps. Mass finished third in the other M23. Back in Europe, Hunt's first victory for McLaren came in the non-championship Race of Champions at Brands Hatch. It was no problem in those lesser races. He also took the Silverstone-based International Trophy, but in the US Grand Prix West he had been out on lap three following a coming together with Tyrrell's Patrick Depailler.

BELOW: James Hunt in the 1976 French Grand Prix at Paul Ricard. Victory there put his quest for the World Championship back on track. *(Ford)*

The World Championship quest had started badly, with only six points from the first three rounds for Hunt, and Mass fractionally ahead of him on seven. Then, briefly, it all seemed to go right for the Englishman. Lauda, in pain with bruised ribs, led the Spanish Grand Prix for many laps, hotly pursued by the McLaren pair. Eventually both got past, and for 31 laps it looked like a demonstration of M23 superiority. Unfortunately, Mass's engine was to blow, but Hunt stayed on to record his first Grand Prix victory for the team… or had he? In post-race scrutineering, the McLaren was found to be 1.8cm too wide across the rear wheels. Team manager Alastair Caldwell remembered: 'We extended the monocoque by mistake by putting the oil coolers in the side. Then we famously got disqualified from the Spanish Grand Prix because we had not measured the overall width. What we had not realised was that Goodyear had made fatter tyres that overhung the rims.' Hunt's disqualification meant Lauda was awarded the nine points for winning. With four races down, the Austrian had scored 33 points, Hunt a mere six.

For a while it did not get any better. The M23 seemed to have lost its competitiveness, mainly because of the repositioning of the oil coolers. Anyway, Hunt failed to finish in Belgium and Monaco, and scored a mere two points for fifth place in Sweden. The team was near to panic; Lauda was up to 55 points, Hunt had progressed to just eight. Caldwell again recalls the nightmare: 'We decided to revert everything to dead safe legal, with the coolers behind the car. There was a rule that said you could not have an oil fitting beyond a certain distance from the centre of the car for safety reasons. Performance dropped off. The oil coolers were then angled, and we tested at Paul Ricard. James said the track

ABOVE: **Did he, didn't he? Hunt was at least first past the flag at Brands Hatch.** *(Ford)*

was just getting cleaner quicker and there was no change. He threw his toys out of the pram when I wanted to put oil coolers back to Jarama specification, but I did and the car was slower. We didn't understand then just how sensitive the wing was to such things.'

However, it was at Paul Ricard and the French Grand Prix that the tide turned. The oil cooler problem had been solved and Hunt was on pole. McLaren gambled on starting the race with part-worn Goodyears, having found that a new set was likely to change its characteristic as the race unfolded. As Hunt recalled, 'Niki set off at a great rate of knots and started to pull away.' He was also, Hunt noted, blowing oil or water from the back of his car. He sat back and waited until on the eighth lap the Ferrari's crankshaft broke. Despite a stomach upset and an urge to vomit during the latter stages of the race, James held on to win, to really win. No official was to take this one away from him, even though his car was minutely examined. That same weekend, FISA (the powers that be) reinstated his Spanish victory, having agreed that the punishment had not fitted the crime. The team was merely fined $3,000, a small price to pay for the return of nine points.

The season had now reached the end of the first points scoring half. There was still a proverbial mountain to climb, but at least the summit was no longer under a cloud. Lauda had dropped to 52 points and Hunt was now in joint second place with 26. By the time the next round, the British Grand Prix, was over and Hunt was relaxing at a barbecue in the Brands Hatch car park with his friends, it seemed to have got even better. James had just won a controversial race in front of an adoring home crowd. Then, as in Spain, they took the victory away and gave it to Lauda… and this time they were not going to give it back.

The capacity crowd was particularly enthusiastic that day. The persona of Hunt, who had just performed on the trumpet to wild applause at the Albert Hall in a televised Grand Prix 'Night of the Stars', appealed to the fans. He admitted that he made a 'lousy start'. Into Paddock Bend the two Ferraris collided, and in the mayhem that ensued, his M23 became airborne. The front suspension was damaged but the car was just about driveable, so he made his way up towards the Druids hairpin before noticing to his delight, particularly as Lauda had escaped unscathed, that the race had been stopped. He accordingly drove down the back road to the pits. With people all over the place, he abandoned it there and ran down the pit lane to his mechanics. His idea was that they would switch his race wheels and tyres on to the spare car for the restart, unaware that

ABOVE: A pivotal moment in the 1976 season – the beginning of the German Grand Prix. Hunt (11) and Mass (12) initially trail Regazzoni's fast-starting Ferrari and Laffite's Ligier. (Ford)

BELOW: Hunt was never really happy with the M26. (Ford)

this was not permissible. The team covered all options, repairing the race car and getting the spare ready. It was the latter that they pushed out on to the grid while the arguments continued as to whether it was or was not eligible.

While the spare was on the grid, the announcement was made that only those cars that had completed the first lap would be allowed to continue. The British crowd was having none of that; the uproar was quite unlike anything ever heard at a UK circuit. Hunt was determined to start, even if they were going to disqualify him. The ruling, if that is what it can be called, now became a little hazy. It seemed now that as long as you were still running at the time the race was stopped you could restart with your original car. With a new steering arm and front suspension link fitted, Hunt's race car was then wheeled out. Controversy seemed to have been avoided. Lauda set off into the lead while Hunt coped with a problem in the left-hand bends because of the way the car had been set up. By half distance, though, he was closing in on the lead. Approaching Druids on the 45th, Hunt dived inside his opponent to take the lead. The crowd was now ecstatic. Their man continued imperiously on to the chequered flag. They little knew of the protests that had been made, that two of the three teams making them had withdrawn them, but that one remained. Significantly, that had been made by Ferrari.

The circus then moved on to the forbidding Nürburgring and an apparent third consecutive victory for Hunt and his McLaren M23. History records that this bland statement hides the lead up to the most remarkable comeback in the history of motor racing. Rain threatened on race day morning, and although the clouds looked as if they might be lifting, all but one of the grid was on wet-weather tyres. The exception was Mass in his home Grand Prix. Hunt wanted to do the same but decided it was wisest to go with the majority. Mass took the lead, with Hunt moving in to second place some 45sec adrift as they completed the second lap. The pivotal moment of the season occurred at about the same time. Lauda's Ferrari had clipped a concrete kerb on a fast left-hander just before Bergwerk. It spun backwards through the catch fencing and cannoned off the embankment back on to the track. By the time the following cars had arrived, the Ferrari was in flames. Drivers Guy Edwards, Harald Ertl, Brett Lunger and Arturo Merzario bravely fought to extract the Austrian, but such were the severe injuries caused through inhaling toxic fumes that his life was in doubt for some days.

Once again a Grand Prix was stopped, but the other drivers were unaware of the extent of Lauda's injuries, believing him to be slightly burned. Following the restart, Hunt virtually had the race won by the end of the first lap, while Mass, having led the first part, finished third. Lauda's lead over Hunt was now down to 14 points as he lay in intensive care. However, an understeering James could only manage fourth in Austria, where Mass tried the under development McLaren M26. Lauda still led 58 to 47. (Gary Anderson, a mechanic with McLaren at the time, recalled that Hunt was concerned about getting out of the M26 with its Kevlar cockpit sides in the event of an accident. Gear changing was also a problem because of the complex routing. It went back into the workshop for further development and did not appear again until well into the following season.)

In Holland, Hunt nipped past the early leader during the early laps, and with the resulting nine points won that day he was right on Lauda's tail. Surely the lead would shortly be his.

Two things conspired against that. The first was that the heroic Lauda was back. Less than six weeks after the Last Rites had been read over him, the Austrian was about to start a Grand Prix. Incredibly, he had only missed two races. There was more drama in Italy, where the locals were, perhaps not surprisingly, hostile to the British driver and team. It got worse when the McLarens were demoted to the back of the grid because their fuel was above the statutory maximum 101-octane limit. Their

times were based on the first, wet-weather, practice session that had taken place before the fuels had been tested. In the race, Hunt was to spin off, while Lauda finished fourth, actually extending his lead – Lauda 61, Hunt 56.

Hunt was in America for the International Race of Champions, a one-make series between top US and Grand Prix drivers, when the next major news broke. He was not five points behind Lauda; he was 17. The Ferrari protest after Brands Hatch had been upheld. The catch-up would have to start all over again and there were only three Grands Prix left, with a maximum total of 27 points available. In quick succession, Hunt scooped up 18 of these, winning both the North American races, while Lauda scored just four at Watkins Glen.

The drama did not let up. Lauda and Hunt arrived in the shadow of Mount Fuji just three points apart. This was the first time a Japanese Grand Prix had been a round of the World Championship; it was to be no conventional showdown. Race day saw persistent rain and the circuit awash. Mount Fuji was hidden in mist. The start was delayed, but when just a hint appeared that the weather would improve, the cars were wheeled out on to the track. 'We should be able to handle a few puddles,' said Shadow's Tom Pryce. Hunt, and especially Lauda, did not, perhaps, see it quite that way. Nevertheless, Hunt shot into the lead and away from the spray. Lauda, who had qualified third, was finding visibility even more difficult than the rest, a legacy of his Nürburgring burns. After

ABOVE: **Teddy Mayer joined McLaren when his brother Timmy drove for the team in the Tasman Series.** (David Luff collection)

BELOW: **Coppuck's final design for McLaren, the M30. Driven by Alain Prost, it scored but one championship point and was invariably slower than the older M29C campaigned by John Watson.** (Ford)

two laps he stopped. There are times when things have to be put into perspective; the World Championship was not that important.

Hunt led, the conditions were improving and the championship was now his to win. However, with two-thirds of the race run, he began to slow down with a deflating left rear tyre. He still had to finish fourth to win the title. Could he afford to spend time in the pits? Team manager Mayer could be wrong whatever he did, so he just left Hunt out. Patrick Depailler went past in his Tyrrell, but then punctured. Mario Andretti (Lotus) took over, but Hunt was still second. Then, thankfully on the final bend of the track, his wet-weather tyre cried enough. He now had no choice but to dive for the pits,

where the mechanics fitted a new set of tyres in less than half a minute. The title hunt was blown; Hunt, now in sixth place, was livid.

In a rage, he hurtled round the closing laps, taking both Clay Regazzoni (Ferrari) and Alan Jones (Surtees). Excitement and confusion mounted in equal amounts as at the finish Andretti, Depailler and Hunt crossed the line almost together in first, second and third places. When the furore died down the onlookers realised that while those placings were correct, Depailler and Hunt were a lap behind the American. Everybody knew, though, that Hunt was the World Champion… except James Simon Wallis Hunt. He was furious, thinking that his race had been mismanaged. Mayer was

GILLES VILLENEUVE AND THE M23

G ordon Coppuck recalled how Gilles Villeneuve's one-off drive in the 1977 British Grand Prix came about. 'There was one thing that was different about James [Hunt] from every other senior driver I have worked with. When it was decided to replace Jochen [Mass], James came into the office and had a chinwag with Teddy [Mayer], Alastair [Caldwell] and myself. He asked, "Who do you think is the quickest guy out there, ignoring me?" We said it had to be Niki [Lauda], so he replied that was the guy we had to have. He was completely confident about who was in the other car. If James had had his way, Villeneuve would have been in the team. He just worshipped Gilles; he told us that we had to have him after he had raced against him in Formula Atlantic at Trois-Rivières. He was so enthusiastic when he came back. I've never had another top line driver who wanted the quickest guy as his partner.

'It was fantastic, that week with Gilles at Silverstone. Teddy was still very nervous of him. During the test day, I think he spun five times but didn't go off the road. Gilles would say, "I was just seeing where the limit was, because I don't know these cars." We were all thrilled with him.'

'I ran Gilles Villeneuve at Silverstone,' added Leo Wybrott. 'James came back from Canada having been beaten by him in a Formula Atlantic race and said that we should sign the guy up. Teddy then arranged for him to come and drive, and we started off with a seat fitting in the factory before going to Silverstone. There were so many cars in Formula 1 at the time that we had to pre-qualify, but Villeneuve was quickest during that session. He was so keen to learn as much as he could about F1 that he would really listen and pay attention. During pre-qualifying we never changed one thing on the car; we used the set up that by then was well and truly sorted, having had the car for so many years. Gilles had a huge number of offs, luckily with no damage, but proceeded to go quicker and quicker. Towards the end of the qualifying we did change some things for him, but not very much. We weren't allowed to have the good tyres to qualify on. We were about fifth at one stage in qualifying and Teddy came down to see what we had done, to see if we had found some magic tweak that we needed to tell him about. There was a quiet confidence about it. Gilles remained at night until we had all gone home, just to stay with the car and learn about it as much as he could. Such a pleasant, likeable young guy.

'The only thing I didn't say to him was that Smith's gauges were temperamental and had a habit of winding themselves off the clock, subjected to a barrage of verbal abuse before he could calmly tell him that he was, in fact, World Champion. Mayer thrust three fingers into the air to indicate his race position had been enough to score the required number of points… just.

Some notable debuts

Despite the fact that it had just been used to win the World Championship for the second time, the M23 was now past its sell-by date. However, both Hunt and Mass soldiered on with the car for the initial races of the 1977 season before the M26 had been developed sufficiently to be the factory's weapon of choice. Hunt went on to win another three Grands Prix with the M26 that year. Even after that, the M23 carried on in privateer hands (see Chapter Seven), taking Tony Trimmer to the British Formula 1 Championship and being used by future triple World Champion Nelson Piquet for his first three Grands Prix.

History, though, had not yet finished with the M23. In July 1977, McLaren entered one, on Hunt's recommendation, for a Canadian Formula Atlantic Series revelation, Gilles Villeneuve, in the British Grand Prix alongside the two regular M26s. One last works hurrah followed when Bruno Giacomelli drove the car later in the year at the Italian Grand Prix.

or the needle would fall off. In the race, Gilles was running well when he saw the water temperature gauge go right round, so he came into the pits. As the B team we were so far down the pit road that I was positioned with the signalling board far from our pit. By the time I got to the car, Gilles had stopped. When you stopped those things from flat out running they boiled instantly and water poured out of the overflow. Stevie Bunn and John Hornby, who were my mechanics, saw the amount of water and assumed that the engine was blown. Gilles had his belts off by the time I arrived. I saw the gauge was blown and sent him straight back out. By then the rest of the field had long gone.

At the time you didn't see the importance of it, but now I realise the privilege of running such a star.'

It was to be Villeneuve's only drive for McLaren, as Mayer decided to sign Patrick Tambay instead. 'I remember vividly the day we tested Gilles Villeneuve and Patrick Tambay,' said Mark Scott. 'Teddy was known for picking the wrong driver. Villeneuve was something like half a second quicker than Tambay, but Tambay did not spin off.

'And then Teddy rang up Enzo [Ferrari] and told him to take Gilles!' added Coppuck. It was motor racing's equivalent of Decca turning down the Beatles.

ABOVE: How could Mayer have let him go to Ferrari? Villeneuve's debut was at the wheel of a McLaren M23. *(Ford)*

Subsequent McLaren history

Gordon Coppuck continued to design the team's Formula 1 cars, with the subsequent M28, M29 and the one-off M30. The latter was not only Gordon's last F1 design for McLaren but was also the final Grand Prix car built under the McLaren name before the effective end of the original company and the beginning of a new operation under former mechanic Ron Dennis, who took over in late 1980. A marriage between Dennis's Project Four Racing team and, a by then troubled, McLaren – which had failed to win a Grand Prix since 1977 – was brokered by Marlboro, who threatened to withdraw their sponsorship if it did not go ahead.

It might be said that the subsequent history of McLaren was that of another company under the same name. The once Kiwi-dominated team was replaced by Dennis's clinical operation, which at times was to dominate Grand Prix racing and which has been one of its leading brands for many decades. Winning ways soon returned following John Watson's victory with a McLaren MP4 (the type numbers had changed to an 'MP' series with the merger) at Silverstone in 1981.

A further eight Constructors' Championships have since been added to that won with the M23 in 1974, while the Drivers' title has fallen to McLaren employees Niki Lauda, Alain Prost, Ayrton Senna, Mika Häkkinen and Lewis Hamilton, ten times since Fittipaldi and Hunt took it with the M23. In addition, the 1995 Le Mans 24-hour race went to a Gordon Murray-designed McLaren F1 GTR driven by an inspired JJ Lehto, partnered by Yannick Dalmas and Masanori Seyika. Given that Bruce himself had, with Chris Amon, won at Le Mans in 1966 with a Ford, it was a fitting result.

RIGHT: McLaren only returned to winning ways when John Watson was the first to take the chequered flag in the British Grand Prix at Silverstone in 1981. *(Author)*

BELOW: Five drivers have won the World Championship with McLaren since the beginning of the Ron Dennis era, the most recent being Lewis Hamilton. *(Author)*

McLAREN M23 GRAND PRIX DRIVERS

The line-up of drivers who competed in Grands Prix with the M23 is impressive. Two, Emerson Fittipaldi and James Hunt, used it to win the World Championship. A further three, Denny Hulme, Jody Scheckter and Nelson Piquet (who thrice raced a privateer M23) had won, or were to win, the world title. At this point, it would also be reprehensible not to repeat the fact that the mercurial Gilles Villeneuve also made his Grand Prix debut with the car. In all, 11 men drove factory M23s, with Hulme, Fittipaldi, Hunt, Peter Revson and Jochen Mass all winning Grands Prix with the car.

Emerson Fittipaldi

World Champion 1974 with McLaren M23. Five Grand Prix wins with McLaren M23 (also World Champion 1972 with Lotus).

While Emerson Fittipaldi did not perhaps show the flair that he had once done with Lotus, his experience brought McLaren its first world title. The Brazilian had moved rapidly through the ranks to join Team Lotus in 1970, winning what was only his fourth Grand Prix and then becoming, what was at the time, the youngest person to win the World Championship in 1972. The following year it was being rumoured that he was looking to leave Lotus. Marlboro wanted him to be driving a car in its red and white livery. By the time McLaren opened negotiations with him, he was already under contract to the cigarette company. It was this that enabled McLaren to afford the sums of money that Fittipaldi now knew he could command. The deal also brought Texaco into the fold.

Fittipaldi's departure from McLaren after two years, having again won the World Championship and a further five Grands Prix to add to his nine with Lotus, was no less dramatic than his arrival. By joining his brother Wilson's unsuccessful team, he effectively ended the glory days of his F1 career. The next five years proved fruitless, and he retired from driving after the 1980 season.

However, a US-based comeback reminded

LEFT: Fittipaldi in conversation with Ronnie Peterson, Belgium 1974. *(Ford)*

BELOW: Having won the World Championship with Lotus in 1972, Fittipaldi repeated the feat for McLaren in 1974. This is him in Argentina the following year. *(Ford)*

the world of just how good Fittipaldi had been. Starting with sports cars, he moved into IndyCar racing and, 14 years after his last world title, took the CART Championship as well as his first Indianapolis 500. A second victory at 'the Brickyard' followed in 1993.

ABOVE: James Hunt
made his Formula 1
debut at the wheel
of a Hesketh-entered
Surtees in the 1973
Race of Champions.
(Author)

Fittipaldi had caused surprise by leaving McLaren to join his brother's team. Hunt and McLaren needed each other.

The Englishman rewarded his new team after a storybook 1976 season by taking the world title with four wins. He stayed with McLaren for another couple of seasons, winning another three Grands Prix with the M26. By 1978 the M26 was no longer a race winner and he left to join Wolf in 1979, before walking away from his uncompetitive drive mid-season.

Hunt was to go on to be a successful television commentator, but his business and private life proved troublesome. Eventually he appeared to have found peace in a life that was far from the high living he had once known, only to suffer a fatal heart attack when in his mid-40s.

LEFT: Hunt in 1976, the year of his championship. *(Ford)*

James Hunt

World Champion 1976 with McLaren M23. Five Grand Prix wins with McLaren M23.

There were a number of potential British World Champions in the mid-1970s, with James Hunt not initially considered to be amongst their number. However, these were still dangerous times and it was the charismatic Hunt who survived to take the title. Teddy Mayer certainly rated highly the man who joined the team for 1976. Hesketh, with whom Hunt had won the 1974 Dutch Grand Prix, had folded and

'Working' for McLaren

Tony Griffiths was employed by Nicholson McLaren at the time. He used a motorcycle to get to work, sometimes riding with Gordon Coppuck. One day the bike broke down near a farmhouse. Griffiths, wearing a McLaren jacket, knocked on the door and asked if he could borrow the phone. He was invited in and offered a glass of sherry. 'My godson works for McLaren,' he was told. Griffiths asked what his name was. 'James Hunt,' came the answer. 'Works for' was one way of putting it.

Denny Hulme

Two Grand Prix wins with McLaren M23 (also World Champion 1967 with Brabham).

Like Bruce McLaren, Denny Hulme had been a recipient of the New Zealand 'Driver-to-Europe' scheme. From Formula Junior, Hulme progressed to Formula 2 with the Brabham factory team. This led to a regular Grand Prix drive in 1966. The following season he became not only a Grand Prix winner but also World Champion with the Brabham-Repco. He also joined his fellow New Zealander McLaren in the latter's Can-Am team, the beginning of a dominating partnership – 'the Bruce and Denny Show' – in the sports car series that was to last until Bruce's death.

The pair worked well together, and for 1968 the forthright 'Bear', as he was sometimes known, became part of a McLaren all-New Zealand driver line-up. Hulme continued to win Grands Prix, the last two of his eight being with the M23. Twice with the McLaren team (1968 and 1972) he finished third in the World Championship. Despite having suffered burns at Indianapolis just prior to McLaren's death, Hulme must be seen as a leading figure in keeping the team together in 1970.

Like Hunt, Hulme was to die of a heart attack, in the case of the New Zealander while driving a BMW in the Bathurst 1000 race of 1992.

LEFT: Hulme's final season with the team was in Marlboro Texaco colours. *(Ford)*

Peter Revson

Two Grand Prix wins with McLaren M23.

Revson, a nephew of the Revlon Cosmetics founder, scored both of his Grand Prix wins with the M23. Although there had been some sporadic World Championship races with a private Lotus in 1964 and a one-off with Tyrrell in 1971, his first full GP season was 1972 when he moved up to McLaren's F1 team to drive the M19. He had first arrived in Europe to race Formula Junior in 1963. The years in between had included sports car and IndyCar racing in the USA and in 1971 he had first joined

LEFT: Revson in Spain, 1973. While a tenacious Hulme won the race, the American could only finish seventh. *(Ford)*

McLaren to race its mighty Group 7 cars, winning the Can-Am Championship, as well as at Indianapolis where he finished second after having achieved the pole.

When it became clear that Fittipaldi would sign for McLaren for 1974, Revson left to join the Shadow team. He was killed in testing at Kyalami prior to the South African Grand Prix. According to his sister Jennifer, 'I do know that he took the [Shadow] ride primarily for the money, as he was planning to retire from racing at the end of the season, though he didn't share that last bit of information with anyone other than his closest friends and family.'

Jochen Mass
One Grand Prix win with McLaren M23.

Mass, who competed in 40 Grands Prix with the M23, justifies his place in the list of those who won with the car courtesy of the truncated 1975 Spanish Grand Prix. An unsafe track and a series of accidents leading to an appalling one when the rear wing on Rolf Stommelen's Hill broke, meant that the race was stopped at 29 laps, which was under half distance. Mass, leading at the time, was awarded the win and half the normal points given for a full race victory.

Mass's Grand Prix career extended from 1973 to 1982, but his years with McLaren were the high point. He was also a leading sports car driver, winning at Le Mans in 1989 with a Sauber-Mercedes.

Other Grand Prix drivers who raced the M23

The early seasons with the M23 often saw three factory cars entered. In the first year, this was to give the team's rookie, Jody Scheckter, a chance. The South African had arrived in Britain in 1971 and immediately showed himself to be a special talent. As one of the few drivers Hulme seemed to have much time for, he earned the nickname of 'Baby Bear'. His other sobriquet of 'Fletcher', named after the main character in the then popular novel Jonathan Livingstone Seagull, reflected his tendency to crash during 1973 in which he drove both the M19 and M23. Indeed, the mêlée that he started at Silverstone that year is perhaps his main imprint on the M23 story. However, he was to go on to prove himself as a Grand Prix winner with Wolf and Tyrrell and then World Champion with Ferrari, once Fittipaldi had indicated he did not want him to stay with McLaren. Phil Kerr was to write, 'Jody was shuffled out of the McLaren team despite his undeniable potential.' In Kerr's

BELOW: Mass's only Grand Prix win was in Spain. The race was massively shortened and he only received half points. *(Ford)*

LEFT: Arguably the greatest motorcycle racer of all time and an undoubtedly brave Formula 1 driver, Mike Hailwood talking to Phil Kerr. *(Ford)*

mind, Scheckter had been an important part of McLaren's future. The experienced Jacky Ickx also drove the third M23 at the Nürburgring in 1973, unsettling the two regular drivers with his speed.

Mike Hailwood, perhaps best known as one of the greatest of all motorcycle racers, with nine world titles and 14 TT wins, also benefited from a three-car set-up. In 1974, having become the recipient of Marlboro sponsorship, McLaren had to run a third, Yardley-liveried, car for contractual reasons. Hailwood, whose Formula 1 career could be split into a period with Reg Parnell Racing in mid-1960s and then three seasons with Surtees in the early 1970s (during which time he also won the European Formula 2 Championship), was hired to drive the Yardley car, scoring a podium place on his third outing with the team. An accident at the Nürburgring later in the season effectively ended his Grand Prix career. The versatile David Hobbs took over the Yardley car for what proved to be the last of his seven Grands Prix.

Two more drivers enjoyed 'one-off' Grands Prix with the M23. Gilles Villeneuve's debut with the car at the 1977 British Grand Prix is the stuff of legend, while Italian Bruno Giacomelli was behind the wheel when the car made its factory swansong at his home Grand Prix later that year.

In addition to the factory drivers, a further

ABOVE: The last person to race a factory-entered M23, Bruno Giacomelli. *(Ford)*

four drivers competed in Grands Prix with the M23. Dave Charlton, who also ran the car in the South African Drivers' Championship, took part in two South African Grands Prix with his version, and Emilio de Villota and Brett Lunger campaigned M23s for part of the 1977 season (and, in Lunger's case, the early part of the 1978 season). Lunger's BS Fabrications car was also used for three Grands Prix late in 1978 by Nelson Piquet. These marked not only the final World Championship events for the M23 but also the first Grands Prix for the Brazilian, who was to go on to win three World Championships. In addition to the above, Tony Trimmer tried, unsuccessfully, to qualify an M23 for the British Grand Prix during that final year.

The designer

Gordon Coppuck

Gordon Coppuck, the designer of the M23, recalled that he was the 13th employee at Bruce McLaren Motor Racing, having been recruited by Robin Herd from the National Gas Turbine Establishment. 'In those days, Bruce always knew what each of us was doing. When he was killed, about 50% of the workforce didn't believe that we would be able to continue. I was in the other half that thought we had learnt enough to keep going. The then Formula 1 designer Jo Marquart was in the other 50%, so we took on Ralph Bellamy to do the F1 and F2 while I did the Indy and Can-Am cars.'

Having already been responsible for the M7C and Alfa-Romeo-engined M7D Grand Prix cars, Coppuck was to pen the fabled M8 line of Can-Am cars, the M15 Indianapolis car and its successor, the M16, which thrice took the Indy 500, as well as the dominant Formula 5000 M10s. 'The M10A was the first car for which I had complete design responsibility. I was starting to know what I was doing,' he said.

The success of Coppuck's designs in North America meant that, when Bellamy left the company, it was obvious who should take over the Grand Prix cars. 'They had confidence in me because we had done all right,' is his masterly understatement.

'For the next Formula 1 design we wondered whether we should build another "coke bottle" shaped car [like the M19] or should we build one like the M16 Indy car. The basic principle of the M16 with a Cosworth DFV engine would be a much lighter package than the M19, so we thought, let's make it like that.

'We ran the first test at Goodwood, but cut it short because we had to get the car off to South Africa. There was only Denny driving it that day and he liked it straight away. He complemented that by then getting his only Formula 1 pole.'

Coppuck obviously has fond memories of this period. 'There was a great camaraderie in Formula 1 in the 1970s. I think motor racing should be fun.'

There are particular memories of the M23's first season. 'The weekend of the French Grand Prix, Peter [Revson] can't drive because he is driving in the IndyCar race at Pocono. So Jody is driving for us. Phil [Kerr] and Jody [Scheckter] decided to reduce Jody's rear wing because the straights at Paul Ricard were so long. He reckoned from the start that he could take the lead on the way down to the hairpin. So, Jody duly got the lead and Emerson got second in the Lotus. Emerson was all over him round the twisty bits. He got so frustrated and ran into the back of the McLaren. Although Jody had led, we still hadn't won a Grand Prix. When he came back from America, Peter was absolutely fuming before the next Grand Prix, which was at Silverstone. He got our bookies' runner from the Colnbrook factory to put £1,000 on his winning the British Grand Prix, having never won a Grand Prix in his life. He duly went on to win the race and a decent bonus from the

BELOW: Gordon Coppuck today with a model of his great creation. *(Author)*

bookmaker for the bet he had placed just because Jody had led the previous race.'

It was many years before Jennifer Revson heard about the betting incident. 'It made me laugh,' she said. 'I have the feeling that it must have been a one-off incident because he certainly wasn't a gambler per se.'

'I was very pleased to be involved in Peter's two Grand Prix wins – Silverstone in fantastic style and Canada, not by luck, you don't win Grands Prix by luck, but in a very confusing race. We didn't know how many laps everybody else had done but we did know we had one more lap to go when Howden [Ganley] thought he had won. He was actually a lap short.'

McLaren later went on to hire, in Coppuck's words, 'a Brazilian with an English temperament and an Englishman with a Brazilian temperament' who between them would give him two World Championships. A particular incident from Fittipaldi's first year with the team stands out in his mind: 'The Nürburgring was an incredible story. Emerson stalled on the grid and Denny ran into the back of him. Denny jumped out of the car, over the pit wall, into the spare car and set off after the field. We were all expecting the black flag at the end of the first lap but to our surprise it wasn't shown, so he did a second lap. Then, of course, it came out. In the modern environment he would probably have been banned for six races!'

Coppuck, who in his time had been a fine

motorcycle trials rider, winning a gold medal in the 1961 International Six Days Trial, was also to design the McLaren M26, M28, M29 and M30 Grand Prix cars before leaving the company to be reunited with Robin Herd at March following the merger with Project Four. Two periods with March were interrupted when he formed the Formula 2 (he admits to a soft spot for that formula) and then Formula 1 Spirit organisation – which reintroduced Honda to Grand Prix racing – with John Wickham. He was also to become part of the Adrem design consultancy and spend time engineering in IndyCar racing.

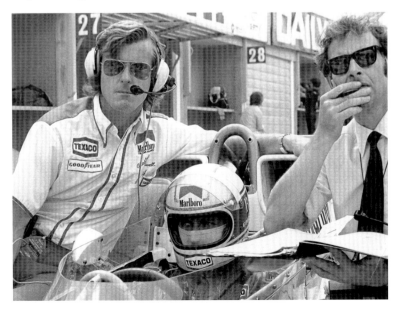

'There was nothing
complicated about it.'

Alastair Caldwell
McLaren team manager

(Author)

Chapter Two

Anatomy
of the
McLaren
M23

The McLaren M23 was one of the
outstanding Formula 1 designs of
the 1970s, having been introduced
to comply with new deformable-
structure regulations. Over a six-
year period it was modified many
times, often in the suspension
area, to successfully retain its
competitiveness. Powered by the
almost ubiquitous Cosworth DFV
engine, it pioneered the use of
the six-speed gearbox and the
compressed-air starter.

Tony Matthews contemporary cutaway of the McLaren M23 shows the car in 1976 guise.

1 Delta-planform rear wing
2 Gearbox oil cooler
3 Rear anti-roll bar
4 Six-speed gearbox
5 Rear beam
6 Inboard rear brake disc
7 Driveshaft
8 Rear outboard coil/ spring damper unit
9 Reversed lower wishbone

10 Roll-over hoop
11 Rear upright
12 Airbox mesh
13 Inlet trumpets
14 Spark-plug leads
15 Cosworth DFV engine
16 Twin trailing arms
17 Exhaust system
18 Third-generation airbox
19 Ring-pull fire extinguisher switch

20 Dry-break fuel filler
21 Medical air supply
22 Side-mounted radiator
23 Fibreglass sidepod
24 Seat belts
25 Seat
26 Cockpit-mounted mirror
27 Cockpit surround
28 Gear lever

29 Quick-release steering wheel
30 Two-part foam
31 Front roll-over hoop
32 Monocoque
33 Fire extinguisher
34 Steering-column universal joint
35 Front rocker
36 Front inboard-mounted coil spring/damper unit

37 Steering arm
38 Front brake disc
39 Front brake caliper
40 Four-spoke wheel
41 Wheel pin
42 Goodyear tyre
43 Brake and clutch cylinders
44 Front lower wishbone
45 Front wing
46 Wedge-shaped nosecone

Tony Matthews

The McLaren M23 was subject to numerous changes over the years, not so much to the chassis, which was one of the stiffest of the time, but more to the suspension. As historian Doug Nye was to observe, this owed more to practice than it did to theory. 'You had a hunch and you tried it.' Emerson Fittipaldi's undoubted enthusiasm for testing also meant that many small changes were made to the car during his two seasons with the team. The M23 was arguably one of the outstanding designs of the 1970s, but the constant alterations mean that the following pages can give no more than a flavour of what happened to the concept during its time in the World Championship.

Like the Lotus type 72, the M23's life was extended by the initial failure of its successor. However, while the Lotus 76 did not reappear, the McLaren M26 did win three Grands Prix after the final retirement of the factory M23s. The career of the more complicated Lotus 72 was one of spectacular ups and downs, while that of the McLaren M23 could be said to have been more even. 'The ethos of the M23 was that it was a very simple car, there was nothing at all complicated about it at all,' said team manager Alastair Caldwell. It was also a strong car. 'I tended to be a bit more concerned with the structural stability of things than my contemporaries,' claimed Coppuck.

Some of the car was carried over from its predecessor, the M19, '…so it was tried and tested and could be relied upon to work well,' recalled project engineer Leo Wybrott.

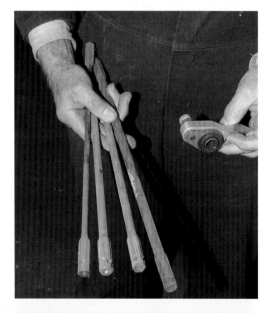

RIGHT: **Kerry Adams shows the variety of front anti-roll bar sizes and an anti-roll bar arm.** *(Author)*

BELOW: **An M23 under construction. The upper inner and outer skins are being installed on the right-hand side.** *(Nigel Beresford collection)*

Specifications

McLaren M23
The car as at launch in 1973.

McLaren M23B
For 1974, the chassis was altered around the front bulkhead to accept alternative progressive-rate or rocker-arm front suspension. Parallel-link rear suspension was also used, and the wheelbase extended.

McLaren M23C
Further revisions were made to the suspension for 1975, and a driver-adjustable front anti-roll bar was fitted. The shape of the airbox was changed and a short nose and side panel extension aerodynamics were tried.

McLaren M23D
A low, regulation airbox was used from the beginning of May 1976. A short-lived driver-adjustable rear anti-roll bar was fitted, as was a longer cockpit surround, which extended on to the nose cone, used to accommodate new signing, the lanky James Hunt. The M23D was also the first to feature the innovative six-speed McLaren-Hewland gearbox and an air starter.

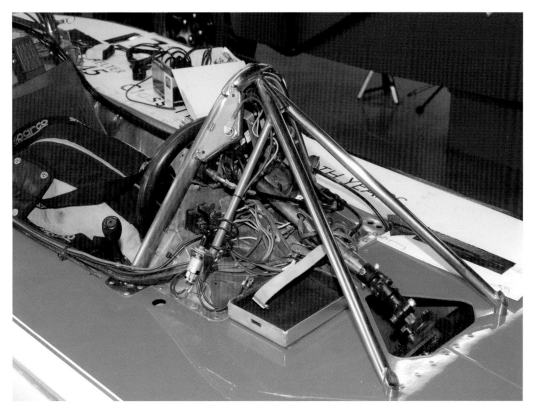

McLaren M23E

Detail changes were made for 1977, including redesigned front uprights to cater for new-diameter Goodyear tyres.

McLaren M23F

This was the specification for McLaren-made parts for sale to M23 privateers.

Chassis

ABOVE: A rear upright on M23/4. Note also the single top link (1) and twin radius rods (2) *(Author)*

Unlike the Lotus 72, which superficially may look like the McLaren M23, the M23 is a straightforward, uncomplicated car. New rules for 1973 stated that the entire fuel tank area of the car in direct contact with the open airstream had to incorporate 'a crushable structure' (see 'Extract from FIA *Year Book of Automobile Sport, 1973*'). Coppuck said that a deformable structure could have been added to the existing M19 but it would have been a difficult job, a bolt-on effort just to meet the regulations. (Lotus chose to convert its type 72s.) Thus, it was decided to create a new car, with fully integrated deformable structure, that followed the spirit as well as the letter of the regulations.

'As this was the first of the deformable structure cars, it meant a lot of development,' recalled project manager Leo Wybrott. 'The fibreglass pods and moulds were all factory manager Don Beresford's responsibility, working closely with Specialised Mouldings. Teddy Mayer was keen that we built the cars as quickly as possible. They went together very well.'

The car was right down to the weight limit when it first started racing. It did grow slightly

BELOW AND BOTTOM: M23/11 has a toggle fire switch while M23/4 has a ring. *(Author)*

RIGHT: A two-part foam is injected into the void between the upper and lower floor skins, using a purpose-sourced aerosol/mixer (on the floor, bottom right). Excess foam bleeds out as the foam expands. Two fabricators stand on a load-spreading plate on top of the chassis ready for when foam is similarly injected into the void between the top of the skin of the chassis and its adjacent panel. There was concern that the foam could distort an unrestrained top outer skin if it did not bleed out quickly enough. Brian Eade is one of those standing on the car, Arthur Willoughby is injecting foam and Don Beresford is overseeing the process, while Gavin Monument is on the far right. *(Nigel Beresford collection)*

heavier over the years, but Coppuck reported that this was kept in hand.

The tub of the M23 was formed in 16-gauge aluminium sheet that was shaped over a large fabricated steel bulkhead at the front and a tank section at the rear, situated between the seatback and the engine bulkhead. The latter featured separate steel fabrications for the top engine mounts. The dash frame consisted of steel bracketry, while steel pick-ups were built in for the rearward legs of the lower front wishbones. The front bulkhead itself extended back 8–10in (203–254mm) into the complex monocoque. All panel joints in the tubs were bonded with epoxy adhesive as well as being riveted, the latter process securing the joint while the adhesive cured.

'We were forever torsion testing our cars. It was obvious that most of the twist was in the cockpit area. I, therefore, decided to make this structural. It was only sheet metal, so if it got damaged you could just unrivet it and put a new one on. There were a lot of M23 copies, but they weren't worth a light because that area was made of fibreglass. We filled the cavity with foam, which also improved the stiffness,' said Coppuck.

The tub tapers in platform and, at the front, in section where the front bulkhead is wider at the top. The radiator sidepods are neatly formed as a delta-form extension that is an integral part of the monocoque. In this the M23 differs from the Lotus 72, which had pioneered side radiators in Formula 1, although in the case of Colin Chapman's design the pods are

detachable. The first Lotus wedge-shaped car had been the gas turbine-engined Type 56 Indianapolis car. In some ways this had been an inspiration for the Type 72, but once Lotus had chosen to have such a shape then the radiators had to be moved from the front. Chapman is also quoted as saying he wanted an increased rearward weight distribution, which could be achieved by side radiators. In the case of the M23 the sidepods also provided two-stage deformable protection. The tub's horizontal skins extend over the pods, shaping into their outer vertical panel. A fibreglass insert section was slid into the pod intake, mating with the aluminium skins and extending into the midship monocoque flank.

After the assembly had been drilled, countersunk and flush-riveted, there was a roughly ¾in (19mm) gap between the GRP insert and the aluminium skin, which was then filled with twin-pack aerosol foam. Leo Wybrott remembered the difficulties of carrying out this task: 'We had to master how much

RIGHT: Radiator inlet ducts (GRP mouldings) have been installed, and the chassis has been inverted and prepared for foaming of this forward chassis side-panel volume. *(Nigel Beresford collection)*

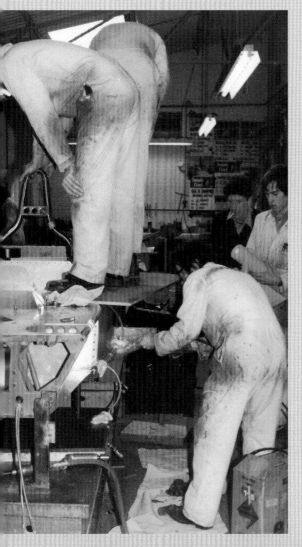

ABOVE: A close-up of the foam injection process being carried out by Arthur Willoughby. The tube dangling down in the middle of the picture is the passage via which foam will subsequently be injected into the upper void. *(Nigel Beresford collection)*

LEFT: The forward chassis side-panel volumes filled with foam. *(Nigel Beresford collection)*

ABOVE: The inner skin has been bonded to bulkheads and is held in place with skin clips while the bond cures, ready to be riveted in place. The steering rack tunnels panel is being positioned and bonded in this photo. The bulkhead was painted with an aerospace-type etch-primer to assist with corrosion resistance and bonding integrity. *(Nigel Beresford collection)*

ABOVE: An earlier
anti-roll bar
arrangement (1) and
an earlier version of
the tubular beam (2)
for the rear suspension
mounting. *(Author)*

ABOVE RIGHT:
The nose mounting
subframe (1) and
battery (2) on M23/4,
also showing the front
anti-roll bar (3). *(Author)*

of the expandable foam we could pump into areas such as the top skin, outer skin and the floor skin. In the delta-shaped sidepod was a female fibreglass section that was pop-riveted to the aluminium outer skins leaving a void of around an inch all around the fuel tank area. It had a male plug that pushed up inside to stop the foam expanding and misshaping the fibreglass. The void had to be filled with foam, and until we worked out how much to use, we had people standing on steel plates above it. We used two-pack foam and a gun with an extension nozzle, doing the whole lot at once. The whole of this build was extremely experimental. We had to cut part of the fibreglass out of the first one because it was so misshapen.'

The front monocoque bulkhead is particularly tidy as all the steering links and arms are behind the front uprights, and only the brake master cylinder and slender front anti-roll bar protrude. For 1974, the front bulkhead structure was modified so that either fixed–rate geometry rocker-arm front suspension or the progressive system used the year before could be fitted.

A tubular subframe extends forward of the front bulkhead. This accepts the detachable nose cone and the front aerofoil aerodynamic loadings. It also carries the lightweight battery,

which was originally supplied to the factory by Varley.

The wedge-shaped nose cone features NACA ducts moulded into each side. These feed slots through the front bulkhead that play cooling air on the damper units.

The fuel tanks are concentrated amidships. The variation in fuel load makes a greater percentage difference to the load carried by the front wheels than by the rears.

Initially, the integral sidepods housed both the water radiators and the oil cooler cores, the one behind the other. During the M23's first race (the 1973 South African Grand Prix) this twin-mounting in the same pod was seen to be a mistake, and the oil coolers were repositioned either side of the gearbox. This resulted in more weight being put on the rear wheels.

The oil tank was located in a recess at the back of the monocoque. The systems catch tank formed a saddle over the bell housing for the transaxle.

New regulations in 1976 set down specifications for mounting oil containers on the car. Prior to the Spanish Grand Prix, small oil coolers had been fitted below the rear wing aft of the transmission. The latest rules required the wing to be moved forward slightly, which meant that McLaren moved the oil radiators to a new position for Spain, just inside the water radiators on the right-hand side of the car. There was concern that this might contravene the regulations, but Teddy Mayer persuaded the authorities that there was a difference in definition between oil containers (or tanks) and the oil coolers that circulated the oil to cool it. Even then, doubt remained and the plan was to return the oil coolers to almost their former position after the race, particularly as the oil had overheated in Spain. In the end, this was carried out in between practice sessions for the Belgian Grand Prix. Because the wing had been moved forward, the coolers were, though, about an inch away from their old placing. This upset the sensitive pressure area under the rear wing and spoilt the airflow, with a resultant detrimental effect on the handling. 'It was horrible,' recalled Coppuck. For the next few races the team struggled until the oil coolers were remounted at the side of the car in time for the French Grand Prix. Having been relegated to almost midfield runner, it was again a potential race winner. Coppuck said that criticism arose over James Hunt because of the above. 'When we put the oil coolers back after Spain we got James to test the car. He could not recognise any difference. But then for two races we were not competitive. The frustration was that he could not tell the difference.'

At launch, the M23's wheelbase was 1in (25.4mm) longer than the M19, at 8ft 5in (2.56m). During its life the car featured a variety of different wheelbases, varying from the initial length to 9ft (2.74m). The first change came about for 1974 when, based on new signing Emerson Fittipaldi's experience with the Lotus 72, the wheelbase was lengthened by 3in (76mm) with a bell-housing spacer extension between the engine and gearbox that set the rear wheels further back. This was done to allow a new rear wing, fitted to comply with new overhang restrictions, to still operate in relatively clean air (see below). The rear track was also widened by 2in (51mm) that year. Coppuck recalled, '[Cosworth boss] Keith Duckworth absolutely hated me. There were two things that he could not tolerate or understand.'

BELOW LEFT: The oil coolers moved around during the life of the M23. *(Author)*

BELOW: The rear wing mounting subframe (1) and anti-roll bar (2) from M23/11. Note the almost infinite wing adjustment and the half-moon rear jacking points (3). *(Author)*

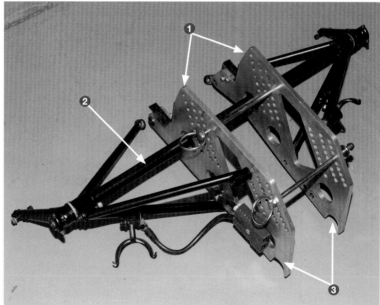

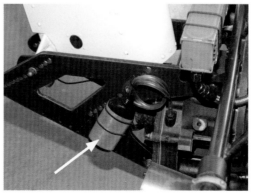

FAR LEFT: Gearbox oil cooler. *(Author)*

LEFT: A less complicated rear wing mounting on M23/4. Also shown is a catch tank (arrowed) for the gearbox breather. *(Author)*

45

ABOVE: **Swirl pot with the top removed.** (Author)

ABOVE RIGHT: **The water header tank.** (Author)

One was the positioning of the fuel pump down the bottom of the front of the engine. That meant we had to set the engine back to accommodate that mechanism. I said I was going to drive it off the top of the camshaft and reduce that wasted area. Also, the thing that spooked the drivers with any Formula 1 car was snap oversteer. While I didn't know how to fix snap oversteer, I did know that if we slowed the reaction down with a long bell housing, that would be something we could do to help. The drivers liked that, so we then increased it by another couple of inches.'

'I don't think the dimension of the wheelbase is important, but it's the way you distribute the weight within the design. You can use a shorter wheelbase at some circuits if you want to. What is important is to have a mass that coincides with the C of G of the car,' wrote Coppuck that year.

At the tight Jarama circuit, McLaren reverted to short wheelbase form; Nivelles was considered ideal for the long wheelbase car, but at Monte Carlo there appeared to be three different wheelbases for the three cars.

The tub was lower than the M19. At launch, the front track was 5ft 5in (1.65m), the rear track 5ft 2½in (1.59m), the overall length 14ft 2in (4.32m) and the claimed weight of 1,270lb (576kg) was distributed 34 front/66 rear. These figures would change over the years. M23/9, for example, featured an appreciably narrower rear track when it appeared at the start of the 1975 season. By 1976, the M23 would be the widest car in the Grand Prix field. That year the rear track was pulled back with what was a new 215cm limit for the Belgian Grand Prix. This was achieved by machining the inside faces and adjusting the wishbone mounting points to match.

The car was lightened by around 30lb (13.6kg) for the 1976 season, mainly through the use of lighter body panels, which were stiffened with carbon-fibre filament. Another way in which weight was saved during the 1976 season was an initiative of Alastair Caldwell's, an idea that was eventually to be taken up throughout the Grand Prix paddock. The idea was to replace the conventional, and heavy, electric starter motor with a compressed-air system that used an onboard reservoir chargeable from any airline and activated by a small solenoid. This meant that it was no longer necessary to carry an onboard battery powerful enough to turn an electric starter. 'We first put the air starter in at Kyalami,' recalled Caldwell. 'The electric starter we had been using was a big, heavy

RIGHT: **A driveshaft from M23/11. Note the splines at both ends.** (Author)

Lucas thing. I thought the obvious thing to do was to use the nitrogen that we carried around to change the wheels. We had this fantastic source of really high pressure. I played with the air tools that we had in the factory. I found a tiny drill would spin a DFV. What I then made was a tenth of the size and of the weight of the electric starter, and the battery could be much smaller. It was a huge gain. I was really stupid because this should have made me a millionaire!'

Aerodynamics

Gordon Coppuck chose a square profile, rather that the round one of the M19, for aerodynamic reasons. Streamlined shape no longer equated to aerodynamic efficiency; what mattered now was that the aerofoils, which had sprung up in the late 1960s, worked well. Unusually for the time, the car was almost fully bodied, with an airbox cowl that merged into

a fat monocoque we had the sidepods that provided the protection.'

'In 1972 we had found the benefit of reducing the angle of wedge on the Indy car,' continued Coppuck. 'I realised we would have a lot less horsepower with an F1 version so I thought we had better reduce the wedge for that a lot. We did use wind tunnels (the best was the Lockheed one at Atlanta, Georgia), so we thought we knew at least where our drag was. This led to the M23 being designed with only one inch of wedge.'

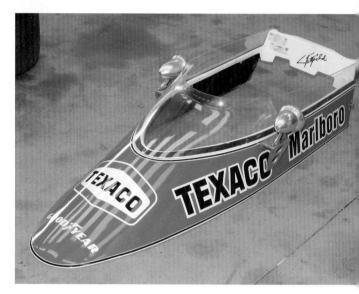

TOP: The M23 features side-mounted radiators like the Lotus 72. This shot shows one of the few curved structures on the car, caused by the crash structure. (Author)

ABOVE AND ABOVE RIGHT: The cockpit surround is fairly high. The mirrors are screen-mounted, two interpretations of this being seen on M23/4 and M23/11. (Author)

the rear tub-cum-sidepod form. This airbox was at first, in the search for cleaner air, much taller than that on the M19. Coppuck observed, 'I think we probably had more downforce than other people because the underside of the car was now very flat. Our drivers never felt intimidated by others on the fast corners.'

It is perhaps not surprising that the side-radiatored M23 bore a passing similarity to the older Lotus 72. 'We recognised that the Lotus 56 jet engine car had been very successful, and we could see that the packaging of the Lotus 72 was that taken to a conventional engine,' recalled Coppuck. 'Thus, we decided that the next car we did would be a side-mounted radiator inspired by the Type 56. However, pencil did not get on to paper for some months after Bruce had been killed.'

Alastair Caldwell added, 'Gordon very cleverly decided to make the sidepods the deformable structure. Instead of having to have

During the course of its life, the wheelbase of the M23 grew from 8ft 5in (2.56m) to 9ft (2.74m). This meant that the rear wing moved further back from the engine, increasing the amount of downforce generated.

During the first test at Goodwood, an M19-style airbox was used simply to cover the trumpets and the tray. A distinctive but bulky airbox was the norm for the first season and up to the 1974 French Grand Prix, when a new slimline version with larger side profile appeared. This extended further back towards the rear wing to improve the airflow on to it. 'To fit the airbox, I bent the injection trumpets inwards. Once again, I was trying to get the airflow to the rear wing. The last trumpet was always the problem in the airbox. You could try to pinch it but you could mess up the pick up,' recalled Coppuck. New airbox rules came into effect in time for the 1976 Spanish Grand Prix. This meant the fitting of a low, ear-shaped affair.

A tubular-strutted rear wing was fitted. 'I was very aware that the airflow to the rear wing was ultra important,' said Coppuck. 'Virtually everybody else had two mounts for the rear wing. On the original M23 I had an aerodynamic-shaped pylon that came up to the wing.'

Caldwell said: 'We took a single, streamlined pillar wing to Kyalami. However, the wing was far too high. I decided to just lower it, which meant it was a lot further back. There was a heated debate about whether this would lift the front wheels off the ground, but it worked like a charm. The car was really steady through high-speed corners; Denny loved it. Everybody then put their wings back in the clean air. It was a "mistake" that worked well.'

The original design had to be modified over the winter of 1973/74 to compensate for the effects of new rear wing overhang restrictions. The rear wing was now 10in (254mm) further forward. As this was measured relative to the rear wheels, Coppuck moved the rear wheels further back. This left the wing in relatively clean air, well behind the airbox (see above). The rear track was also widened to minimise interference from tyre turbulence.

Following early season races in South America, Coppuck and his team began to experiment. A clever new wing mounting was tried that was drilled on various arcs, which enabled a wide range of alternative wing incidences to be used. A pointed 'winkle-picker' nose was also tried, which carried longer span, high-aspect ratio front foils with exaggerated banana section. It very much changed the car's wedge appearance but was short-lived, only being used in practice at Monte Carlo in 1974 complete with long-span front foils. M23/5 had tall, vertical masts fitted on the foil tips. 'We did this narrow nose for Spain and Monaco. At Monaco, Emerson said that he had lost sense of where the front wing was, so we had little pylons fitted. Perhaps we got the idea from hill-climb cars. We were looking to see if there was more lift on the nose than there was downforce for a longer wing, but it didn't change anything,' said Coppuck.

In 1974 at Dijon-Prenois, vertical plastic skirts around the under-periphery of the car were tried, but they quickly wore away on contact with the track. The idea was to exclude air from the underneath of the car and so minimise lift and allow the wings to apply downforce more effectively. Work on the Can-Am cars had given Alastair Caldwell ideas about downforce, and so he had suggested plastic skirts on the M23. The nose frame was made loose so that the wing could lift up, otherwise, under heavy braking the nose would touch down and downforce would be lost. 'We cut a hole in the floor underneath the driver and we measured with a pitot tube, finding that we had

ABOVE, LEFT AND BELOW LEFT: **There were three different airboxes during the life of the M23. Gordon Coppuck revived the low 1976 version for the March 871, leading James Hunt to joke, 'So this is what you did with my airbox!'** (Author)

ABOVE: A winkle-picker nose was tried at Monaco. Hillclimb-like stalks were fitted to the wings so that Fittipaldi could see the corners of the car. *(LAT)*

RIGHT: The nose, which was wider than that of the Lotus 72, featured a highly cambered front wing. *(Author)*

a decrease in pressure underneath the car. We had more downforce without more drag and the car went just as fast on the straight; it was a free lunch.'

Two years later, skirts were tried again in practice at Kyalami, but they were taken off following a protest that revolved around wing heights and what was the underside of the car. 'We had a day off and I went out to ride motorbikes. When I returned, Teddy [Mayer] had taken the skirts off. I asked why, and was told that Colin Chapman and Ken Tyrrell had said that they were going to protest. I put them on again for the next race and the scrutineers came to me, but I told them that the rules said you could not have moveable aerodynamic devices. I said these do move but I don't move them, God does! This argument about what was moveable and what wasn't went on for many years.'

While McLaren had returned to the earlier wedge shape of nose for 1975, these were abbreviated when the cars appeared at the

start of that year. At the 1975 Dutch Grand Prix, M23/9 sported rearward sidepod extension panels to improve further the airflow over the rear wing. A new, swallow-tailed rear wing was fitted to Fittipaldi's car shortly afterwards, although the Brazilian's win at Silverstone when it was first used had far more to do with his ability in treacherous weather conditions. New contoured flairs on the trailing edges of the radiator pods were fitted for Germany, where the plastic skirts also reappeared.

ABOVE: An earlier single-element, highly cambered rear wing on M23/8. *(Author)*

LEFT: A second-generation airbox being positioned. *(Dave Luff collection)*

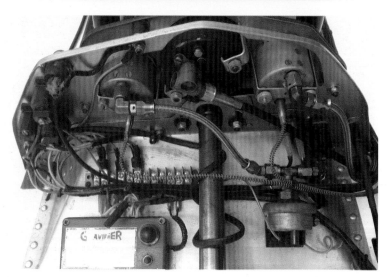

ABOVE LEFT: The dash of M23/11 with later front roll-over hoop. These became mandatory halfway through the 1976 season. *(Author)*

LEFT: By contrast, there is no front hoop on M23/4. *(Author)*

BELOW LEFT: The back of the dashboard on M23/2. *(David Luff)*

ABOVE: Signing up the tall Hunt meant that the pedals had to be moved forward on his car. *(Author)*

RIGHT: Willans belts in M23/4. Having driven the car at Goodwood, Emerson Fittipaldi has left his mark. *(Author)*

Cockpit

The cockpit of the M23 is much cooler than that of the M19, thanks to the repositioning of the radiators and the fact that the large fuel tank behind the driver insulates him or her from the heat of the engine. Lack of a nose radiator and this tank mean that the driver sits further forward than in previous McLaren F1 designs, with feet ahead of the front axle line. However, the space is as confined as possible, this having been done to narrow the tub and ease the airflow into the hip radiator ducts. When James Hunt joined the team for 1976 the pedals had to be moved forward in his car to accommodate his length. 'When we first went testing with James at Silverstone, he could not fit into the car,' remembered Caldwell.

The steering box is inboard of the front bulkhead, just ahead of the dash panel and under 12in (305mm) from the steering wheel.

Hunt wrote that the instruments were 'pretty irrelevant' during a race. However, the M23 was originally fitted with Smith gauges for fuel pressure (0–160psi) and water temperature (30–120°C), a chronometric tachometer (0–12,500rpm) with telltale, plus dual oil pressure (0–160psi) and oil temperature gauges (30–120°C).

The fire extinguisher (originally Graviner) is located crosswise beneath a panel under the driver's legs. After the extinguisher in Mario Andretti's Lotus 78 exploded during practice for the 1977 Argentine Grand Prix, Hunt requested that his extinguisher bottle be either removed

ABOVE: Jochen Mass's helmet connected to a medical air supply. (Nigel Beresford)

LEFT: The gear lever of M23/11. (Author)

BELOW: A modern SPA 'FireSense' fire extinguisher underneath the cockpit of M23/4. (Author)

or emptied. However, despite the fact that he pointed out the extinguisher could only cope with a minor electrical fire, he was told that this would contravene the regulations.

In 1975, Fittipaldi's car was fitted with a cockpit adjustable front anti-roll bar, which enabled him to soften roll-stiffness as his fuel load diminished. This was removed for the German Grand Prix.

The M23 was one of the first Grand Prix cars to feature a quick-release steering wheel. Since 1971 a regulation had been in force concerning the ease with which drivers could escape from the cockpit, and the narrowness of the cockpit made this virtually impossible without this feature.

RIGHT: The quick-release steering wheel coupling as seen in the 1970s. *(David Luff collection)*

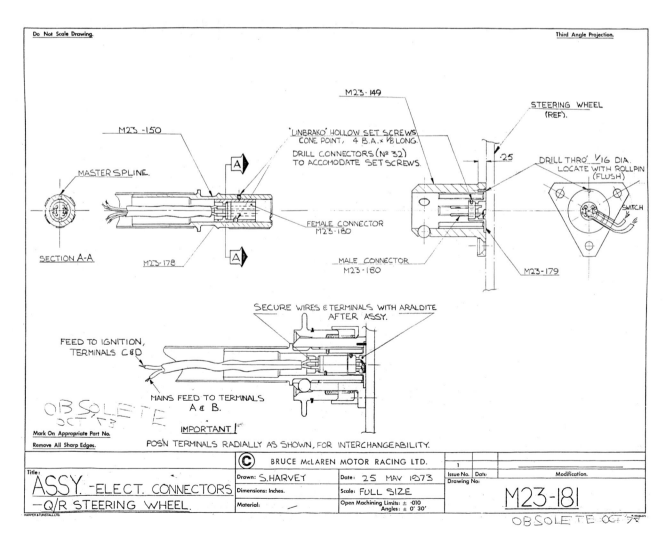

LEFT: M23/8 retains a period steering wheel. *(Author)*

ABOVE: The distorted steering wheel from Mike Hailwood's Monte Carlo crash in 1974. *(John Hornby)*

Suspension

The original M23s carried over the tried and tested rising-rate front suspension of the M19, which facilitated a lower front ride height. 'The front suspension is basically that of Ralph Bellamy's design,' wrote Gordon Coppuck in *Autosport* during 1974. 'It was very good, and the advantage of it was by arresting the car over any bumps.' Under braking the suspension would become progressively stiffer and reduce the car's tendency to dip. Its most significant aspect was that it never actually went solid.

The system, which gave a cleaner airflow to the side-mounted radiators, comprised wide-based lower wishbones and triangulated tubular top rocker arms, whose inboard extremities compressed the inboard spring/damper units via linkages with rising-rate geometry.

The rising-rate suspension was far from simple. Even former McLaren mechanic Kerry Adams, who has since become noted for restorations of his former employer's cars quipped, 'I didn't understand the rising-rate suspension. When I rebuilt Jody's M23, I had to call up Ralph [Bellamy] to ask him how it worked!'

Chief mechanic David Luff also remembered the initial front system. 'The M23 had masses of different front suspensions, but it started with a version of the M19's which was known

as "winky wanky" suspension. It was not easy to work on as it had two tiny links that were less than an inch-and-a-half long. The length was quite critical. You could change the rising rate [by adjusting the length of these linkages]. When it started life at ride height it might be 275lbf/in. When the chassis started going towards the ground it increased the rate. Today you would buy a spring that would do the same thing.'

ABOVE: The rising-rate front suspension and tubular top wishbone was initially carried over from the M19. Here it is seen on Jody Scheckter's M19 in Kerry Adams's workshop. *(Author)*

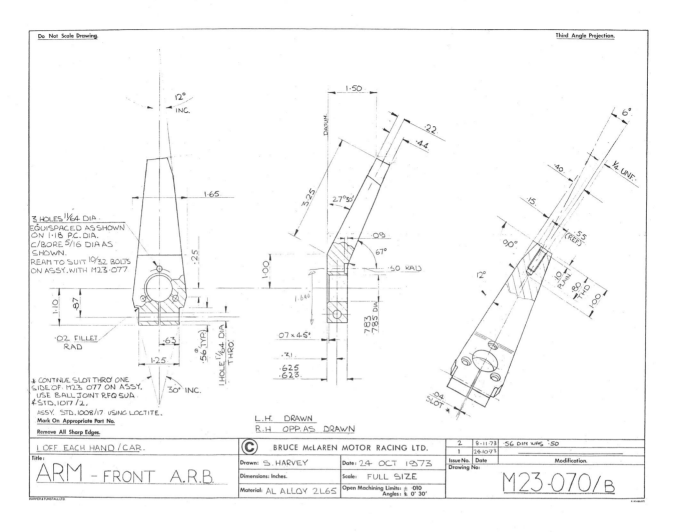

3 HOLES ¹¹/64 DIA.
EQUISPACED AS SHOWN
ON 1·18 P.C. DIA.
C/BORE ⁵/16 DIA AS
SHOWN.
REAM TO SUIT ¹⁰/32 BOLTS
ON ASSY. WITH M23·077

·02 FILLET RAD

✳ CONTINUE SLOT THRO' ONE
SIDE OF. M23·077 ON ASSY.
USE BALL JOINT RFQ SUA
✳ STD. 1017/2.
ASSY. STD. 1008/17 USING LOCTITE.
Mark On Appropriate Part No.
Remove All Sharp Edges.

L.H. DRAWN
R.H OPP. AS DRAWN

1 OFF EACH HAND / CAR.	© BRUCE McLAREN MOTOR RACING LTD.		2	8-11-73	·56 DIM WAS ·50	
Title:			1	24-10-73		
ARM – FRONT A.R.B.	Drawn: S. HARVEY	Date: 24 OCT 1973	Issue No.	Date	Modification.	
	Dimensions: Inches.	Scale: FULL SIZE	Drawing No.			
	Material: AL ALLOY 2L65	Open Machining Limits: ± ·010 Angles: ± 0° 30'		M23·070/B		

HARPER & TUNSTALL LTD.

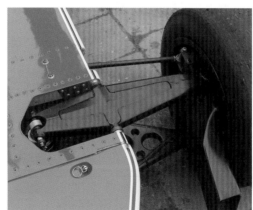

RIGHT: The later front rocker system seen on M23/8. (Author)

FAR RIGHT: Front inboard-mounted coil spring/damper unit activated by the upper rocker arm. Note the anti-roll bar link (arrowed) connected to the rocker arm. (Author)

RIGHT: An original-style rocker on M23/2. (David Luff)

LEFT: Rear outboard coil spring/damper unit mounted directly to the cast upright. Note also the reverse lower wishbone (1) with single top-link (2) and twin radius rods (3). *(Author)*

LEFT: This shot of the rear suspension shows the driveshaft splined at both ends. *(Author)*

Experience with the M19 showed that the variation in fuel load and the difference between the load carried by the front wheels and that by the rears with a midship fuel tankage allowed for a simpler system to be used with progressively wound coil-springs, which became coil-bound from the lower end as load increased.

Reversed lower wishbones, adjustable top links and twin radius rods were used at the rear. The bumpy bankings at Interlagos meant that optional higher radius rod pick-ups were used there in 1974.

At launch, the M23 had its own front upright package, but such as the axle and wheel bearings were from the M19. The rear uprights had a sliding axle so that the driveshafts were of fixed lengths. The floating axle system used two needle roller bearings that floated sideways in and out of the upright as the suspension rose and fell, a system used on the M19. The wheel face prevented the shaft pulling through one way while the fixed universal-joint yoke prevented it pulling through the other way. This worked well and, opposed to conventional sliding-spline driveshaft joints, saved unsprung weight. This was further saved when titanium driveshafts, with steel yokes pushed on to them, were used.

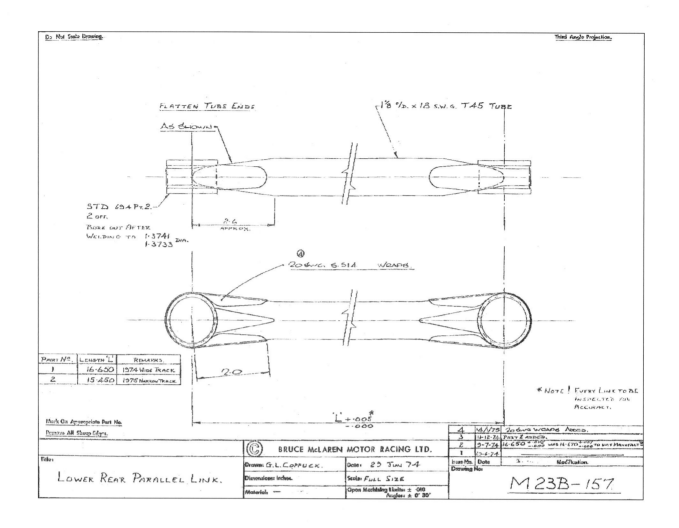

FLATTEN TUBE ENDS

AS SHOWN

STD 694 Pt.2.
2 OFF.
BORE OUT AFTER
WELDING TO 1·3741
1·3733 DIA.

1⅛ O/D. × 18 S.W.G. T45 TUBE

2·6
APPROX.

④ 20 G.W.G. 6.51A WRAPS

PART Nº	LENGTH 'L'	REMARKS
1	16·650	1974 WIDE TRACK
2	15·450	1975 NARROW TRACK

Mark On Appropriate Part Nº.

Remove All Sharp Edges.

2·0

'L' +·005 *
   -·000

* NOTE ! EVERY LINK TO BE
INSPECTED FOR
ACCURACY.

4	14/1/75	20 G.W.G WRAPS ADDED.	
3	11-12-74	PART 2 ADDED.	
2	9-7-74	16·650 +·015 WAS 16·670 +·035 TO SUIT MANUFACT	
1	23-6-74		
Issue Nº	Date		Modification.
Drawing Nº			

© BRUCE McLAREN MOTOR RACING LTD.

Title:
LOWER REAR PARALLEL LINK.

Drawn: G.L. COPPUCK.   Date: 23 JUN 74

Dimensions: Inches.   Scale: FULL SIZE

Materials: ——   Open Machining Limits: ± ·010
                  Angles: ± 0° 30'

M 23B – 157

BELOW: 1973-style front…   **…and rear suspension on M23/2.** *(David Luff)*

At Jarama in 1974, M23/6 featured five alternative lower and three alternative upper pick-ups for the rear radius rods in order to research optimum anti-squat characteristics. 'This year we tried a lot of anti-squat experiments,' wrote Coppuck at the time. 'Emerson liked it.'

The M23s were modified after Mike Hailwood's crash at the Nürburgring. The lower front wishbone pick-up point was strengthened to stop the steel fabrication punching through the side of the inner monocoque wall, which is what damaged Hailwood's leg.

When the eighth chassis was built in 1974 it featured low-offset front suspension with revised steering geometry, which reduced steering effort, and parallel-link rear suspension, like the then current version of the Lotus 72.

Early in 1975 various suspension revisions were tried to improve front-end adhesion. The ninth chassis, which appeared at the start of that year, featured front suspension in which the original tubular front rocker arms had been replaced by swept-back, sturdier, fabricated top arms with pull-rods under their outboard extremities. These pulled up a shaped actuating arm at the foot of gently inclined semi-inboard coil spring/damper units.

This suspension, which owed much to Brabham, was modified by the time the car went to Kyalami. Right-angle (instead of swept-back) arms were installed, which helped lengthen the wheelbase and put less load on the front wheels. M23/6 was also prepared with this suspension, while M23/8 was fitted with the swept-back pull-rod front system. A third variant was tried once the team was back in Europe. The pull-rod experiments had proved unconvincing. At the International Trophy at Silverstone, Jochen Mass tried a non-rising-rate fully inboard front suspension that then became standard. The coil/dampers were mounted totally inboard again, but this time vertically, and actuated by conventional fabricated steel top rocker arms.

'With the M23 we were learning all the time,' Coppuck reflected. 'We now got our rising-rate off the bump rubber with less weight.'

'It seemed like we were changing geometry every weekend,' recalled Kerry Adams. 'That probably wasn't really the case, but it just seemed like it at the time. Gordon would come up with a new design and say it was wanted for the next weekend, so there would be people cutting and welding different geometry designs. We were obviously trying to improve the car and, as we know, it went past its sell-by date but was still competitive. We certainly saw the change from rising-rate suspension to rocker suspension as being the way forward. It was certainly simpler to work on; the rising rate was a bit "fiddly".'

Another way in which weight was trimmed for 1976 was the reappearance of reverse lower wishbones at the rear. The parallel-link rear suspension had worked well but had been heavy. Toe-steer was controlled by the accurate setting up of the radius rod lengths during build. The joints at each end of the radius rod were screw-adjustable for length.

ABOVE: **A rear bump adjuster on M23/2.** *(David Luff)*

BELOW: **M23/2's rear suspension beam.** *(David Luff)*

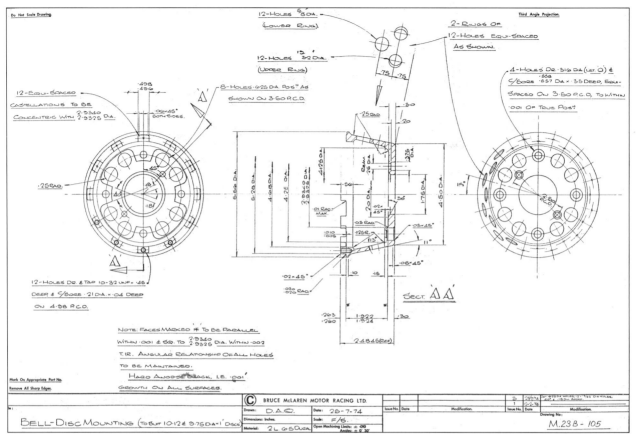

Brakes

McLaren's dominant time in the Can-Am series is perhaps reflected in the Lockheed four-pot brake calipers that were fitted, these having been developed for the Group 7 sports racers. These clasped 10½in (267mm) ventilated discs all round. The discs were mounted outboard at the front – where live stub axles were used – although not buried within the wheels. At the rear they were mounted inboard, thus further reducing unsprung weight.

The inboard rear brakes made sense because of the driveshaft, but Coppuck chose not to go inboard at the front. Nevertheless, the car, relative to its time, was clean through the front corner. Gordon is very adamant about not having front inboard brakes, referring to the fact that McLaren driver Denny Hulme was behind Jochen Rindt, whose Lotus 72 had inboard front brakes, when he was killed during practice for the 1970 Italian Grand Prix. 'I didn't believe

RIGHT: The front caliper is attached to the leading edge of the upright as the steering arm is on the rear edge. *(Author)*

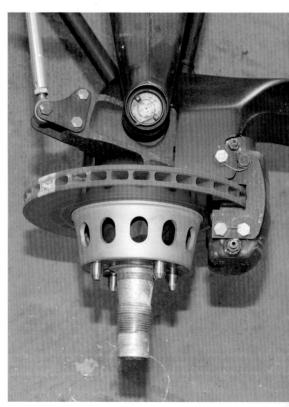

in them myself but the internal politics would have gone through the roof if I had suggested them. I didn't like the car being as wide as it was and inboard front brakes would have made it even wider.'

At Long Beach in 1976, the cars were fitted with Can-Am brakes with a 35% greater pad area than before.

A problem with the brake pads was that they would taper, leading to the driver complaining about a 'soft' or 'long' pedal. The mechanics had to make sure that they would always go back in the same position, always assuming that new ones were not being used. A soft pedal could also be caused by the brake fluid getting too hot, which necessitated bleeding the system.

Wheels and tyres

The four-spoke 13in x 11in (front) and 13in x 16–18in (rear) wide wheels were also carried over from the M19 and remained the same diameter throughout the life of the M23. They were made from a casting by Kent Alloys. McLaren would then X-ray them for porosity and potential cracks, while Ultraseal Slough, a specialist in impregnation services, would also treat them.

ABOVE: Avon tyres are now fitted for historic racing. However, Goodyear was the supplier to the factory during the 1970s. *(Author)*

ABOVE RIGHT: Avon on M23/8. *(Author)*

BELOW: As in 1973, Goodyear tyres are still fitted to M23/2. *(Ford)*

Because of the flexibility of the tyres and the inability of the tyre bead to stay on the rim, McLaren fitted four securing bolts, with domed heads and Dowty sealing washers through the wheel to stop the tyres from coming off the rims.

The sole tyre supplier to McLaren during this time was Goodyear, although any M23 currently being used in historic racing has to use the spec Avon A11 compound. A wide variety of compounds and construction were used. Once Goodyear had fitted a tyre, the McLaren mechanics would subject them to a leak test, using a watering can. The tyre pressure that the car would start the race on would be well below that recommended,

as the heat that built up would increase the pressure. David Luff remembers that if the required pressure were 16psi, the team would start the race with about 11psi.

Qualifying tyres were used in the 1970s with compounds that were rated from A to D. The latter were literally good for one lap before they became badly blistered and would have to be thrown away.

The front tyres were 20in, while the rears ranged from 26in to a one-off 30in. Twelve months after its debut at Kyalami, the M23 was fitted with new 28in outside-diameter Goodyear tyres on the 13in rims for a test at Paul Ricard. 'It was like a dragster with ripples on the sidewall,' said Coppuck. 'The traction was phenomenal and the lap times weren't bad. Denny said you would go into a corner and wait for the sidewall to take effect, and then the grip was very good. However, the regulations changed and then it was not possible to use such a tyre.'

Engine

With the exception of M23/2, which was briefly fitted with a Leyland V8 to compete in the Formula 5000-based Australian Drivers' Championship, all the McLaren M23s used the water-cooled 2,993cc Cosworth DFV 90° V8 engine. This had been introduced in 1967 and, during its first season, was used

ABOVE: This shot of Mass's car at the 1975 British Grand Prix shows the airbox removed and the mesh above the injection trumpets. *(Ford)*

FAR LEFT: The exhaust system was typical of its time. *(Author)*

LEFT: A Cosworth DFV sump/lower crankcase. *(Author)*

exclusively in the Lotus 49, winning on its debut at Zandvoort.

Quoted in John Blunsden's and David Phipps's early book on the DFV, *Such Sweet Thunder*, designer Keith Duckworth pointed out that he never considered making anything other than a V8, despite the fact that most rivals 'seemed to think that 12 cylinders was the absolute minimum for a 3-litre Formula 1 engine'. However, Duckworth reckoned that the mechanical efficiency of a V8 would be better than that of a 12-cylinder – leading to improved fuel consumption – and that it would be easier to keep weight down. Repco had already proved what could be done, by winning the 1966 and 1967 World Championships

with a simple Oldsmobile-based sohc V8, although it was helped by the unprepared nature of its rivals.

By the time the M23 was introduced, it was the engine of choice in Formula 1, vindicating Duckworth's conviction that more cylinders still were not necessary. At the 1973 South African Grand Prix, 20 out of the 25 cars on the grid made use of the DFV, including Denny Hulme's new McLaren. In 1967, power output was claimed at 400bhp. Power improvements made in 1971 – to a typical 450bhp at 10,000rpm – were considered good enough to carry the engine through a couple more seasons, a period when the M23 was introduced. However,

suffered from the torsional vibration troubles
of its early days. McLaren itself introduced
a variety of improvements. During the early
days of the M23, McLaren's engine arm,
Nicholson McLaren, introduced the first short-
stroke versions of the DFV. John Nicholson
remembered: 'During the time of the M23
there were all sorts of changes, mainly dictated
by the team, probably Alastair [Caldwell] or
Gordon [Coppuck]. Trumpets were tweaked
in, pumps moved and welded. The engine had
found an extra 20hp but the cam profile did not
change until the late 1970s. By now we were
doing engines for more than McLaren, and
everybody had their own way of doing things.
Parts like magnesium water pumps would only
last one race.

'The initiative to introduce the short-stroke
version came from ourselves; Teddy [Mayer]
and Phil [Kerr] just wanted more development.
We wanted to put bigger valves in the engine,
and to do that we needed bigger pistons.'

by the time James Hunt beat Ferrari's Niki
Lauda to win the World Championship in 1976,
Cosworth had rated the output of its DFV at
465bhp at 10,500rpm.

Subtle changes had been made to the DFV
by the time the M23 appeared, and it no longer

Block

The Cosworth DFV is based on a light, asymmetric, LM 8-WP heat-treated aluminium alloy cylinder block with a five main bearing crank. The alloy was reasonably easy to cast and had excellent machining properties. The blocks were cast in Worcester at Cosworth's own foundry, where the company employed a special casting process that enabled it to produce an aluminium block that matched the strength of a cast-iron one. The block extends from the decks to the centreline of the crankshaft, the lower half of the crankcase being integral with the sump casing.

The front, centre and rear main bearing caps are formed by the sump/lower crankcase, and numbers two and four bearings have conventional bolted caps. The caps are aligned with one dowel either side and are tightened regularly so that the gap between cap and block remains square. When this is achieved the dowels are locked, the feeler gauge is slid out and both sides are slowly torqued. A hole underneath the metering unit allows for any leakage (such as fuel or water) going through the right-hand cylinder bank.

Cylinder liners

Using an aluminium block meant that, at the then stage of metallurgical development, it was necessary to fit cylinder liners. The originally wet cast-iron liners in each of the cylinders are in constant contact with water. The inner bore is perfectly straight. The liners are sealed by two O-rings at the bottom and Cooper's mechanical joints at the top. The block should be cleaned and prepared prior to fitting the liners and all marked for the correct position within the block, which should be heated to 150°C to receive the liners. The liner must be a certain distance from the top of the block. Sealing between the cylinder head and the block is secured by a Cooper ring located in a recess formed between the liner and the block. Grooves machined on top of the block at the edge between the liner give an indication of leaks. In the event of a blow-up, the liners can be changed by keeping the standard bore and machining its location in the block to accept a bigger external-diameter liner.

Having originally purchased liners from

ABOVE: **The block.** *(Author)*

LEFT: **A cylinder liner.** *(Author)*

BELOW: **Flat-plane crankshaft.** *(Author)*

Cosworth, McLaren's engine arm (Nicholson McLaren) changed its supplier to MAHLE.

Crankshaft

The nitrided M 40B steel forged crankshaft is of a flat-plane shape, mounted low to keep the centre of gravity low. At one end, a boss takes the flywheel with eight 3/8in UNF bolts. On the other is the location for the timing gear. The crankshaft revolves in five, steel-backed main bearings with lead indium wear surfaces, with conventional bolted bearing caps for numbers two and four bearings, the remaining caps integral with the sump/lower crankcase. It has five journals, and four pins with two con rods mounted on each pin next to each other. On the timing gears side, the crank gear drives the series of gears; the main gear is secured via a press fit and located on one dowel. Conventional oil seals are used, secured on the flywheel side by a retaining ring. On the front of the engine, the oil seal is pushed in the front timing gear cover and secured by three screws.

ABOVE: Con-rod, piston, rings and gudgeon pin. The crown of the piston was elevated to raise the compression ratio; hence the dimples for valve clearance. *(Author)*

Pistons

The forged light-aluminium pistons are retained on the con rods in each case by a gudgeon pin, which is retained by two circlips. Between pin and circlips are dished synthetic washers known as Belleville washers. The piston crown is pocketed to give clearance to the valves. Three piston rings are used, two compression and one oil control ring. As with the liners, Nicholson McLaren changed its supplier from Cosworth to MAHLE.

Connecting rods

The design of the con rods and the pistons followed the same lines as the Cosworth FVA Formula 2 engine. The con rods are steel forged, split across the big ends at 90° to the rod shank, the outside being shot-peened for extra strength. In the little end there is a mixture of soft metal alloy. On the big end there is a plain shell bearing held by a cap and two 3/8in UNC high-tensile bolts. The tightening of the con rods is conventional.

Cylinder head

The light heat-treated aluminium alloy cylinder heads have aluminium, bronze and copper-nickel valve seats and guides. The heads are interchangeable between the cylinder banks. The inlet ports are inclined towards the centre of the engine on both cylinder banks, the exhaust ports to the outside. The ports to each combustion chamber merge into a single inlet tract inside the head. On the front of the cylinder head is an idler gear that drives the camshaft gears mounted on a roller bearing on a steel pin that protrudes from the cylinder head. All the valves are assembled with double springs. These are held to the valves by a top cap with two collets. The valve stem is sealed to the guide by a rubbery seal held against the valve stem by a spring. This, in turn, is held on

ABOVE: Timing gears from the front of the engine. *(Author)*

RIGHT: The head with valves and springs fitted. *(Author)*

to the guide by the bottom spring platform. Ten studs hold the cylinder head to the block, four smaller studs on each outside edge. There are two 1.36in (34.5mm) diameter inlet valves and two 1.14in (29mm) diameter exhaust valves per cylinder, with 32° included angle and 0.41in (10.4mm) lift.

Cam carrier

The cam carrier is retained by ten pairs of studs, that also retain the cam bearings, and eight cap screws. The cam carrier carries the tappet pistons and camshafts in its own assembly. A small shim is located between the valve stem and tappet bucket. Both shims and buckets are made from steel.

Camshaft

The two per cylinder bank, steel, gear-driven overhead camshafts run in five plain shell bearings secured by caps, which are numbered to avoid being incorrectly replaced. While the inlet and exhaust cams are the same shape, they cannot be wrongly installed because of the distance between the lobes arising from the different diameter of the inlet and exhaust valves. At the front end and rear of the front bearing is a shoulder that prevents the camshaft from moving longitudinally. On the back of the engine is a magnesium plate held to the cylinder head by four ¼in UNC bolt cap heads and a 5/16in bolt drilled for pressure relief. Another magnesium plate is bolted to the cam carrier in like fashion. These seal the rear of the cylinder head and the cam carrier.

The cam cover is cast in magnesium and bolted to the carrier by 22 10/32in UNF cap head screws around its edge and ten 5/16in nuts and washers down its centre. The front part of the cover is designed to form part of the engine mounting. Four 5/16in bolts secure an engine plate to the cover, which is bolted to

the chassis by a single 3/8in UNF bolt. An aluminium mounting block is located at the bottom of the sump and bolted to the chassis by two 3/8in studs.

To lubricate the cam, an oil passage passes through the cylinder head from the block to the centre camshaft bearing. The camshaft being hollow, this allows the oil to pass to the other bearings as well.

Throttle slides

The throttle slides rest on a series of rollers and ball bearings, the guillotine travel being limited by plastic stops. The guillotine is returned by two springs located on the back of the manifold and supported by two plastic plungers. These springs are aided by two additional ones that are mounted to suit different throttle/pedal arrangements.

ABOVE: **Camshaft.** *(Author)*

LEFT: **Camshaft bearing caps.** *(Author)*

ABOVE: **Throttle slides – one closed, the other open. The slides had an advantage over butterflies, as when on full throttle there was no restriction to the airflow into the engine.** *(Author)*

Inlet trumpets

The conical-shaped inlet trumpets are supported by the manifold top, as is the throttle control rod. They are mounted on two O-rings and retained by a steel ring that is screwed to the manifold top. The fuel injector is screwed into a boss in the trumpet.

Metering unit

The metering unit and the electrical assembly are connected to a small gearbox that obtains its power from the second compound gear via a quill shaft. This means that the timing of the ignition and fuel injection can be accurately set in relation to each other. The unit is located inside the V, the front of the metering unit being supported by an aluminium mount bolted to the block.

Looking from the front, the layout of the timing gears follows the shape of the engine. The crankshaft gear drives the first compound gear, which in turn drives the second compound gear. This provides the take-off point for the metering unit/ignition assembly drive and carries on the timing gear to the camshafts via idler gears. The second compound gear is a complex assembly made up of a hub incorporating 12 miniature torsion bars. At the end of the line are the camshaft gears, bolted to the camshaft by three cap screws. These gears are enclosed by a cast magnesium cover on the engine and also two smaller magnesium covers on each cylinder head assembly. On the left-hand side are the mechanical fuel pump, the water pump for the left-hand bank and the oil pressure pump. On the right side is the water pump for the right-hand bank and the scavenge pump. Between the rear of the water pump and the front of the scavenge pump is a small clutch assembly that will slip at a pre-set load, thus preventing damage to the rotors and front drive belt when the oil is cold.

Water pumps

The two centrifugal water pumps, one each side of the crankcase, are identical in construction apart from the fact that they are left- or right-handed and therefore cannot be interchanged. The impeller is contained in the aluminium housing of the pump body, and its shaft is supported by two ball bearings. Water from the pumps is passed through an aluminium tube secured to the block by a cast aluminium elbow. The tube is sealed to the elbow and to the pump outlet with rubber O-rings.

Oil pressure pump

The oil pressure pump body is mounted to the engine. It contains the rotor, pressure relief valve and oil filter in one assembly. The pumping mechanism is a conventional eccentric rotor type. Oil is passed from the pump to the engine via a pipe, excess oil from the pressure relief valve being bled into the scavenge system. The pump receives its power through an Oldhams coupling from the rear of the left-hand water pump.

Engine oil system

Oil is drawn from the tank into the oil pump, where it is pressurised and pumped through the filter into the cylinder block via a steel tube. It passes through oil ways in the block to the crankshaft assembly, the cylinder heads and camshaft assemblies, with a small amount being directed on to the compound gears through a small jet. It returns to the sump and is scavenged and returned to the tank via oil coolers. The oil tank is vented to a catch tank.

Water system

The water pumps are connected by a passage in the sump that enables water to be introduced into either pump. The water is pumped by the impellers in the cylinder block, passes around the liners and through the cylinder head, leaving the engine through an outlet at the rear of each head. It returns to the pumps having been cooled through the radiators. A thin aluminium cover protects the belt and pulley arrangement.

Fuel system

An electrical high-pressure pump sucks five-star petrol through a filter, which goes to a non-return valve or bypasses the mechanical engine fuel pump, then to another filter and the metering unit that distributes the fuel to the cylinders through injectors.

Fuel injection system

Use is made of the indirect Lucas shuttle metering system. A separate electric pump is mounted on the chassis and governed by a dashboard switch. This sucks the petrol from the tank, sending it around the system. The petrol is pressurised, and the pressure is controlled by a relief valve designed to keep the pressure at around 110psi. The fuel is fed to a metering unit, which combines a metering distributor with mixture control. A piston, driven by the shaft, coming from the distributor located inside the metering unit, sends the correct amount of fuel at the precise time to each cylinder. The amount injected is determined by the travel of a small free piston or shuttle operated by the fuel pressure. The mixture control assembly comprises a fuel cam mounted on the front of the unit and liaised to the slide by a rod. When opening, the slide determines the travel of the shuttle, sending the quantity of fuel to be injected. The engine also receives the exact amount of fuel to match the quantity of air admitted. The metered fuel reaches the cylinders through injectors located on the outside of the trumpets, which atomise the fuel as it enters the air stream. The shuttle or fuel cam is mounted on an eccentric pin going through it. This has five positions and initially is set in full rich position when cold. A different set of fuel cam profiles is available to suit varying racetracks.

BELOW: The fuel filter. *(Author)*

BELOW MIDDLE: The mechanical fuel pump on M23/3. *(David Luff)*

BOTTOM: The scavenge pump on M23/2. *(David Luff)*

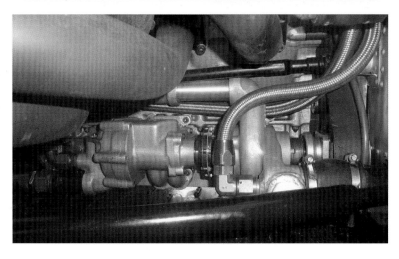

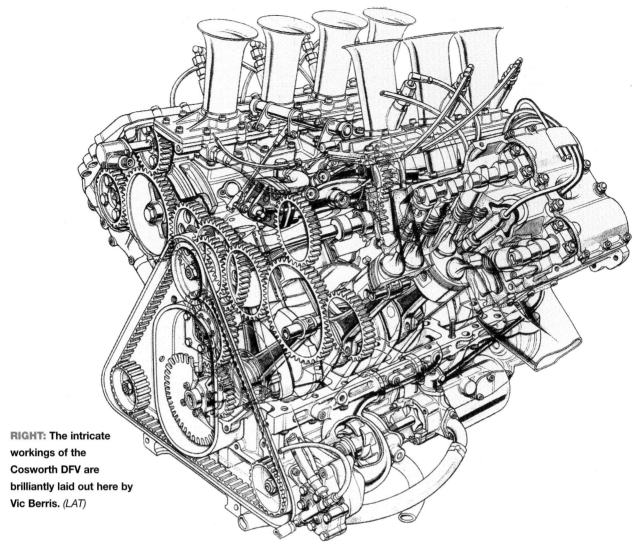

RIGHT: The intricate
workings of the
Cosworth DFV are
brilliantly laid out here by
Vic Berris. *(LAT)*

Cosworth DFV engine specification

Configuration: 90° V8
Capacity: 2,993cc
Bore: 3.373in
Stroke: 2.555in
Compression ratio: 11:1 (approx)
BHP: 480 (approx) at 10,500rpm
Torque: 245lb/ft at 8,500rpm
Valve lift: 0.410in (less tappet clearance)
Timing: Inlet 102° MOP
Exhaust 102° MOP
Firing order: 1-8-3-6-4-5-2-7

Cylinder configuration:

Front	
5	1
6	2
7	3
8	4
Rear	

Cylinder block: Cast aluminium alloy.
Wet liners: Cast-iron in constant contact with water.
Crankshaft: Steel. Turns on five main bearings. Positioned between block and sump.
Con rods: Forged steel (shot-peened).
Pistons: Forged aluminium with two compression rings and one oil control.
Ancillary system: Two water pumps, one per side. One oil pressure pump. One scavenge pump.
Cylinder heads: Cast aluminium alloy, two 1.14in exhaust valves x two 1.36in inlet valves per cylinder assembled with double springs. One spark plug per cylinder located in the centre of the combustion chamber.

Inlet manifold: Cast aluminium alloy inlet trumpets, press-formed steel with injector location.
Cam carriers: Cast aluminium alloy takes the tappet piston and camshaft.
Throttle slides: Steel sliding on a series of ball bearings and rollers returned by two guided springs.
Camshafts: Four steel (each turns on five bearings).
Cam covers: Magnesium casting.
Injection systems: Lucas indirect injection shuttle metering system. Pressure 110psi approx. Injection timing at 30° ATDC.
Ignition system: Lucas OPUS ignition with thyristor engine speed limiter. Lucas alternator.
Spark plugs: Champion R56 or equivalent.
Weight: 165kg

LEYLAND V8

John McCormack installed in M23/2 a racing version of the 4.4-litre aluminium V8 that Leyland of Australia had built for the large Leyland P76 saloon, which was only available in that country. This was an enlarged derivative of the Rover V8 that had been originally designed as the Buick 215. The car was run in this format from 1976 to 1978, and reduced in size to a 4-litre for the Can-Am Challenge. However, Leo Wybrott then rebuilt it back to conventional specification with a DFV. All the McLaren M23s now have DFVs installed, as when built.

The lone M25, which made use of a Cosworth DFV during its pseudo M23 days, was initially fitted with a 5-litre Chevrolet V8, as befitted its Formula 5000 origins. When it was rebuilt back to original specification, a Chevrolet V8 was again installed.

Gearbox

Initially, the McLaren M23 was fitted with a standard (by then well-sorted) Hewland FG400 gearbox. This five-speed box was by then common for the Cosworth DFV-engined Formula 1 cars, having replaced the heavier Hewland DG300. The FG400 was basically a combination of this and Hewland's FT200 Formula 2 gearbox, using a slightly different casing. Many of the FT200's features had been retained, including the gears with larger DG final drive parts. (The M25 made use of a Hewland DG500 five-speed box during its time as a Formula 5000 car.)

At Interlagos in 1976, McLaren introduced an innovation for Formula 1, a six-speed gearbox. 'By this time we were getting so sophisticated that we had a specialist gearbox man, John Hornby,' said team manager Alastair Caldwell.

The advantage of the six-speed box was that the engine could be kept in the most effective rev band, within a range of about 2,000rpm. While the Cosworth DFV could keep up with Ferrari's power unit on the straights, it was at a disadvantage when it came to all-round torque. Coppuck recalled that the object with the six-speed box was to make the most of the useful engine speed range.

LEFT: The rear of the six-speed box on M23/11 removed for ratio changing. (*Author*)

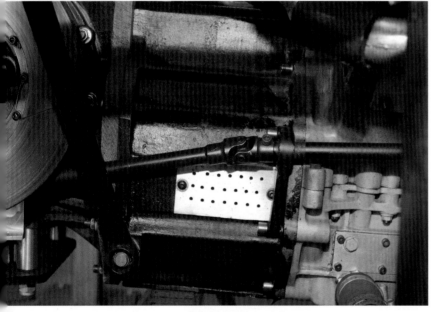

Grands Prix, said, 'To be able to work on these cars is quite awe inspiring.' He admits, however, that it can now be difficult to acquire parts for the 'box.

'I designed the six-speed conversion for the gearbox, which was a major breakthrough,' recalled Caldwell. 'Up to then, most of the conversation at a debriefing would be about the gear ratios. James [Hunt] used it for the first time in Brazil. I remember clearly at the evening debriefing after practice, when he had taken pole, we talked about the handling, about the brakes. After about an hour I asked what about the ratios? The drivers replied, "Ratios?" They had no idea which gears they were using, it was like night and day. They said they were just using the right gear.'

Hornby said, "We had to remove the reverse gear idler on the front of the gearbox main case, then spot faced the gearbox in order to allow the larger diameter first gear to go right up against the bulkhead. We changed the first and reverse gear hub to carry first speed with a turned round second gear hub. So, first gear now was where reverse gear had been. We changed the fork on the selector rod and the selector rod because of the detent, changing to a conventional fork to carry a conventional dog ring. Then the rest of the 'box was built up as normal but with six speeds. This then gave us a problem with reverse gear, which then had to be squeezed into the finger housing at the back. We had to get one gear on each shaft, which made the layshaft nut the actual gear, with splines on the pinion to carry another small gear on the finger housing side of the bearing. We then introduced a reverse idler gear on a selector fork. We put a post in the back face of the bearing carrier and drilled the rear cover to support it, putting it into double shear. We squeezed it in with the fingers in line for the selector finger to pick it up when reverse gear was required. This meant modifying the detent plunger by putting two steps on it so that first gear position could be felt before pressing down to get reverse.'

'You can't select reverse easily, as McLaren made a longer detent spring and a longer plunger,' observed WDK's Hoad.

'Ken Tyrrell was convinced that we did not

ABOVE TOP: Layshaft from the six-speed box. (Author)

ABOVE: The gear linkage used solid rods as opposed to the cables later in use. (Author)

'Alastair came up with the idea of the thing,' said Hornby. 'He came down into my little workshop and started playing around with hubs and taking a few measurements inside the casing. He didn't at first say what he was thinking, but he then got me involved in getting the first gear sorted out, and the oil pump. McLaren then did all the development and the thing worked well from day one.'

Even today, the McLaren six-speed gearbox is to be admired. Gearbox technician Jonathan Hoad, who works on Charles Nearburg's M23 at WDK Motorsport, and was not even born when the M23 raced in

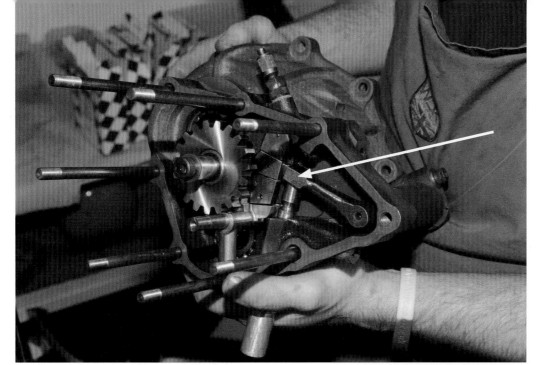

have a reverse gear, so this had to be proven on several occasions,' said Hornby. 'Because of the size of reverse gear, it was all too easy to break, as Alastair once demonstrated in the workshop.

'We did away with the oil pump drive off the layshaft, so we had to reposition the oil pump. This we did by machining the inside of the gearbox main case and putting an extra spline on the input shaft to drive a gear, and then machined up a little oil pump which went into the rear, right-hand corner of the main case, held in position by a banjo bolt. These were tricky things to make, so out of seven gearboxes we only had five oil pumps.

'We never bought a complete box from Hewland, we just used to buy bits.' A year after McLaren, Hewland built its own, heavier and longer, six-speed gearbox. McLaren also tested a sequential gearbox in an M23 with Fittipaldi in 1975. 'It wasn't perfect,' remembered Caldwell, 'and, because we were so busy, we didn't go back to it.'

A problem with the six-speed box in the tight cockpit was, observed Hornby, 'either that the position of the gear lever caused the driver to bang his hand on the side wall of the car or bash it on to his leg trying to get first or reverse. Thus the logical thing to use was a sequential gear change, but we had lack of development time and the mechanism was not up to the job.' It would be a long time before a sequential box would be used in Formula 1.

ABOVE: Cosworth DFV components awaiting assembly on the bench at Nicholson McLaren. *(Author)*

When the McLaren M23 made its debut at the 1973 South African Grand Prix, Cosworth DFV engines powered 20 of the 25 starters. The DFV was to remain numerically dominant during the M23's active Grand Prix lifetime. However, while still using the DFV, McLaren had already taken its engine destiny into its own hands.

John Nicholson had become part of McLaren's Kiwi nucleus in 1969, initially working on V8 Chevrolet engines. 'Then Cosworth dropped a bombshell by saying to the Formula 1 teams that they needed to get their own engine boys because they could not keep up with the manufacturing of new engines, development and servicing. At the end of 1970, I was asked by Teddy [Mayer] and Phil [Kerr] if I would take on the Cosworth work. I had expected to be back in New Zealand by then, but it paid for the tax on my new Ford Capri, so I stayed!

'For the next couple of years I employed three or four boys and we had a very small part of 17 David Road [then McLaren's factory in Colnbrook]. We could only build a couple of engines at a time. Up until this stage Cosworth would not allow anybody, even if they owned the engine, to take the lid off it. I don't know what Keith Duckworth's logic was.

'Having now got one apart, we did not know where to start. Cosworth certainly did not help, and it took us about a week to get it apart. Things were just pressed together and you had to know where everything went. After a week I went back to Cosworth with a long list of questions, expecting answers, but all I got were a few clues. We were on our own and had better just get on with it.

'We made use of the Champion spark plug company's dyno at Heathrow and slowly but surely got the engines running. We had no drawings and we had to make tools for everything. But, I'm a DIY Kiwi, so what the hell?

'In 1971/72 we were building about 50% of the team's engines, maybe more. Any new engines bought by McLaren during those years would still have to be serviced by Cosworth. We were pretty pleased after those couple of years, but the interesting thing was the unbelievable variation in the power output between engines. The best one was number

061, which had 460hp on the Champion dyno, while the worst one had about 420hp, yet everything looked identical. However, by the end of 1972 McLaren was looking for serious development. I told Phil that we needed a proper workshop to do this. Within less than a week he had found a new factory in Green Lane. It was Phil that chose the name Nicholson McLaren for the company, not me. I was most surprised by it. It took about six months to get a dyno up and running, but we were still able to use the Champion one.

'As we learnt more, so we were able to improve the engines quite considerably. We changed to MAHLE pistons and liners. Cosworth knew, all of a sudden, that we weren't buying pistons from them.

'Of course, we won the championship in 1974 but by then we had done our first short-stroke version. We achieved 500hp that year – 499.6hp to be precise. I'll never forget that. There was also a lot of headwork that went on. It was easy to break through into the water jacket with the improvements that we wanted to make, so we had to slow down, but we knew what the engine was capable of. Later there was an improvement in the castings.'

Nicholson was not just an engine man. Driving a Martin Slater-designed Lyncar, he won the 1973 and 1974 British Formula Atlantic titles. He then commissioned Slater to build a Formula 1 example powered by one of his own engines for the following season. He started the Brands Hatch and Silverstone non-championship races that year, but failed to qualify for the British Grand Prix. In 1975 he made it on to the grid for the Grand Prix, finishing 17th. He was eventually to move on to power boat racing. In 1980 his company, Nicholson McLaren, became independent of McLaren International.

BELOW: John Nicholson competed in non-championship Formula 1 using a one-off Lyncar, naturally powered by one of his own engines. (Author)

LEFT: John Nicholson heads the Nicholson McLaren team in the 1970s. (John Nicholson collection)

'It would tell you what it was going to do before it did it.'

Emerson Fittipaldi
Marlboro Team Texaco driver
1974 and 1975

(Ford)

Chapter Three

The driver's view

Although Emerson Fittipaldi believed the Lotus 72 was a better car than the McLaren M23, there is no doubting how much its drivers appreciated it. More straightforward and arguably safer than some of its contemporaries, they knew that they had a winning car. Fittipaldi made it his own during his time with the team, but that did not stop James Hunt from also taking the World Championship with it.

The McLaren M23 appears to have been appreciated by all who drove it. Denny Hulme is said to have liked it immediately. William Taylor, in his book *McLaren*, quotes him as saying, 'It oversteers and stays out there in a nice, comfortable slide.'

When the team signed Emerson Fittipaldi for the M23's second year, Hulme was content to leave all the testing to the enthusiastic Brazilian. 'Consequently,' he wrote in *Autosport* that year, 'I had nothing to do with the '74 version.'

The fact that Fittipaldi was, as he admitted, obviously the team's number one driver, did mean that Hulme's relationship with the M23 suffered. At Interlagos in 1974, 'the car was the most terrible thing I have ever driven. It was really a bad car. I think some of it was due to the way the car had been set up because Emerson had made all the tests, and it was due to the tyres and the way they were working.'

By Jarama, Hulme was happy with the car again, but it was obvious that the M23 was being developed to suit Fittipaldi's very different driving techniques. Despite the New Zealander's quote above, Emerson preferred to drive the car more on the throttle with the tyres sliding, while Hulme preferred slight understeer. It had been very different in the car's first year, when Hulme and Revson could easily jump into each other's cars and immediately feel at home. The fact that the T-car was also set up for Fittipaldi did not help Hulme either. Hailwood also had a T-car that year, but the Yardley team was run as a separate operation.

It was not always love at first sight, as it had been with Hulme. In his collaboration with Eoin Young, *James Hunt Against All Odds*, Hunt wrote, 'When we got to Brazil [in 1976] it was all wrong... it didn't fit me, the steering wheel was too heavy and I didn't like it.' That was just the first day, during which the team simply went about setting the car up for its new signing. That meant, amongst other tasks, cutting into the front bulkhead and mounting the pedals ahead instead of behind it. It would not be long before Hunt changed his mind about the M23.

RIGHT: Denny Hulme liked the M23 immediately. *(Ford)*

Emerson Fittipaldi

'The first time I tried an M23 was at Paul Ricard on the short circuit,' recalled Emerson Fittipaldi. 'The car was extremely fast. It was nearly flat by the end of the straight. I was surprised by how smooth the car was. It had very good brakes. It was not too quick to change direction at the esses after the pits. We worked on this for a few days. By the end of the test I was doing some very competitive lap times.

'You could have a lot of confidence in the car. It would tell you what it was going to do before it started to do it. It was a simple car to work, much simpler than the Lotus 72. It was a great car. One of the best I ever raced. I had a very efficient relationship with the team – Teddy Mayer, Alastair Caldwell and Phil Kerr. The M23 was perhaps not as good as the 72, but as far

as team strategy going from Grand Prix to Grand Prix, and developing the car, McLaren was better organised than Team Lotus. It was very pleasant to work with the whole team. Ninety per cent of the crew seemed to be New Zealanders.

'At McLaren we had to work from Grand Prix to Grand Prix, trying to adjust the car to set it up for the track. We had three different wheelbases, three different sizes of spacer between the engine and the gearbox. For some of the shorter tracks we tried a shorter wheelbase car and it worked.

'In the Argentine Grand Prix we had a very fast, long corner. The car was superb there. I was doing a good race, and then I decided to switch off the car! I braked for the hairpin, the engine died and I stopped on the grass. We had no radio then and I wondered what

ABOVE: **Hulme in the south of France, 1973.**
(Ford)

had happened. Then I saw I had knocked the steering-wheel-mounted switch off with my finger. We made a protection for that for the Brazilian Grand Prix! We worked hard in Brazil to make the car work. It was extremely good in all the fast corners at Interlagos. The old track there had a lot of them. I lost time, though, on the slow corners – they were a difficult part for the McLaren.

'Then Goodyear changed the tyres. By the British Grand Prix, Gordon Coppuck (working with John Barnard who was then a junior engineer) made a new rear suspension. Brands Hatch is very bumpy, there is a lot of weight transference from front to rear. The M23 could be very difficult on bumpy tracks. We made a big improvement in the car.

'The 1974 Brazilian Grand Prix stands out. Interlagos was a very difficult and bumpy track but we got the car working really well there. Another was at Monza where I was sandwiched between two Ferraris (Niki and Clay). I had a hard time after the race from the Italian crowd.

'I remember one of the first times I saw a McLaren M23 going fast was Jody Scheckter at the British Grand Prix in 1973. He made a big strike! I was second or third at the time with the Lotus. Jody was very fast into the fast corners. The McLaren was extremely good through the fast corners like Woodcote.

'I think the new geometry, fitted from the 1974 Brands Hatch on, helped to win the championship for sure. In 1975, again the car was extremely competitive. I think I twice had engine failure and I lost the chance to win the championship. Normally I would again beat the Ferraris. There was not much difference from the previous year, but there were some developments like an aero nose for Monaco that gave more downforce on the front, and we played with the wheelbase again, and different wings. We not only made the car shorter but we also put more weight on the rear, then made it longer and put more weight on the front. We even played with wide track at the front, and there were a lot of different airboxes.

'The 1975 British Grand Prix was my last Grand Prix win. I saw the clouds coming and I was thinking it is going to rain very heavily.

I went by Copse and then I had drizzle on my visor, so I said I am going to stop and put on wets. I was the first one to come in. By the next lap the storm was not yet that heavy. Then on the following lap I came to the main straight and there was zero visibility, but I was still flat out as I was on wet tyres. Suddenly I see the back of a car just going very slowly and I missed by this much [Fittipaldi indicates the smallest of margins with his hands]. I was full speed, perhaps 180mph and the other guy was doing about 60mph. I just saw the shade of the car and saw it was Mario Andretti in the Parnelli... on slicks! He was on his way into the pits. Afterwards I say, "Mario, I didn't know if I was going to kill you or you were going to kill me."

'When they stopped the race, I was leading. I think 12 cars I saw crashed at Copse, everyone had spun into the catch fencing. It was my last Grand Prix win.'

BELOW: **Fittipaldi enjoys the fruits of victory at Watkins Glen 1974.** *(Ford)*

Jochen Mass

'I came from Surtees, which was my first experience [of Formula 1],' said Jochen Mass, speaking on the set of the film, *Rush!*. 'We had the TS9, which was quite good, then we had the TS14. It wasn't basically a bad design, but lack of funding meant that it was not engineered in an appropriate fashion. Then I came to the McLaren, which was obviously a better car. However, from the sheer feel of it at first there was not such a great difference. It was not like stepping into a miracle machine that enabled you to do whatever, but it was a quick, solid car and it was quick if you knew how to set it up and what to do with it. The basic underlying quality was just better than the Surtees. You could do more with it and it was very forgiving.

'It was a wonderful car but you had to work with it; there was no way of just sitting in it and being super quick. That did not work; in those days you really had to make the most of it. Everything – the ride heights, the wing settings, the tyre pressures – had to be made to suit your driving style. It did not like understeer, it did not particularly like oversteer but it was nice to be able to transfer the weight to the back. The M23 allowed you to do all that, while with some other cars you could not because

of sheer fault of design. The McLaren had a broad spectrum of possibilities, but it could also give you a headache.

'Emerson once asked Teddy, "What do we do tomorrow if it rains?" Teddy replied, "Don't worry, just panic."

'The M23 was a fine car but it probably was not the very best, the Lotus 72 might have been a little bit quicker. The McLaren, though, was more rationally built. Gordon Coppuck did a fantastic job with that thing. He wanted to make it safe and reliable, and these are the key things in Formula 1.

'You always started with a full fuel load and there were no tyre changes so you had to make the car quick at a certain time in the race; towards the end you should gain a little bit. However, the car was damn good on full tanks and did not fall off, so it was a pretty manageable machine, an all-rounder. That was probably its biggest strength. Full or empty, it was always quick.

'The Nürburgring, when I led, I was driving on slicks and I managed to keep it on the road. I had a big lead and then the race was stopped and I finally finished third.

'Another one was Jarama, where I caught up to James and was lying close behind him. I had already worked out where I should overtake him – without hurting anyone – it was always difficult with teammates! Then the engine blew up for no apparent reason.

'The first lap at Interlagos: Andretti led but I overtook him down the straight so I was leading. At the bottom end of the straight the road broke up. I braked late and could not stop. Everybody else was warned looking at me, but I spun off and hit the Armco quite hard. You don't always want to be first!

'1975 could have been a good one at the Nürburgring. We had tyre problems, and the Goodyears all broke. We hardly did more than a lap on one set of tyres. They brought in a planeload of fresh ones from the United States. They mounted three new ones, and the front right was an old one. Why, I do not know. On the first lap I was lying fourth down the Foxhole and I thought, "I can win this one." It felt good and the Nürburgring was always my favourite. Then the front right delaminated completely. The whole tread came off, flop, flop, flop, flop. A left-hander came up, I could not brake hard. I braked gingerly and then hit the Armco on the right side of the road, skied along the barrier and then went across the road where I got stuck in the catch fencing. The spectators looked down and one yelled, "Idiot, can't you go slower on the first lap?"

'We had very sensitive aerodynamics. A little example: I was screwing around in qualifying at Kyalami and the car was always different, never the same. It just didn't seem to handle right. I came in and said to the guys, "There must be something wrong." They replied, "Yeah, yeah, where were you last night?" I went out again but I just could not get a time. I came back in again and then James came in. Then they said, "We've found something." I asked, "What?" but they said they weren't going to tell me, and I said that I had heard that before. However, they did something very quickly and sent me out. Immediately I got third fastest time. It was just the Gurney flap that was fixed on the sides but not in the middle. It really did 'flap'!

'Keith Duckworth said to me long after I had left Formula 1, "You guys never had a chance. Three teams had evolution models – Tyrrell, Lotus and McLaren – and guess who got them, Scheckter, Andretti and Hunt. They had at least 50hp more." James was a brilliant

driver, but he wasn't necessarily quicker than I was, and I knew that.

'When I heard about the *Rush!* film, I felt that I should be doing something in it because I was very much part of 1976. So, I was asked if I could drive on a few occasions. The engines now have a lot more power.'

Jody Scheckter

' I drove the McLaren M19 first,' recalled Jody Scheckter. 'The M23 was a little faster, but it's not easy to compare. [By comparison] when I then went on to Tyrrell I didn't like that at all. Driving in the McLaren team was fantastic.

'There were drivers with plenty of experience [in the team] that they shared, but Denny didn't tell me everything. At Paul Ricard he was using first gear at the hairpin and he didn't tell me, but then I went quicker than him in practice. I only did one warm up lap while the others did two. I was on the middle of the front row, with Jackie Stewart on pole, but when we got to the first bend I saw that he was in my mirrors.'

ABOVE: **Jody Scheckter's own McLaren was on display at the 2012 CarFest held at his Laverstoke Farm.** *(David Luff)*

SCHECKTER'S BIG MOMENT

The McLaren team could only watch aghast as Jody Scheckter lost control of his M23 at Woodcote on the first lap of the 1973 British Grand Prix. Mayhem ensued as a vast proportion of the field crashed in his wake. Four interested parties recalled the incident.

Alastair Caldwell:

'Scheckter was our new boy and Denny, who used to hate other drivers, loved him. He talked to him a lot about the car. Denny was about fourth going into Woodcote and he saw Scheckter behind him. The kid got a left front wheel on the grass and, to his great credit, never lifted. He would have crashed anyway if he had. You could hear him trying to get it back but he failed, spun and hit the pit wall right under our feet. There was complete carnage. It wrote off nearly half the field, including the whole Surtees team. I remember John attacking me physically. I was saying, "John, John, I didn't drive the car!"'

Gordon Coppuck:

'I had brought Jody and his parents to the race in my car because we both lived in Camberley. He T-boned the wall and somebody went between him and the wall while a BRM clipped his rear wing. I was so pleased that Peter won and then got himself a decent bonus from the bookmaker.'

David Luff:

'Jody took out most of the field! It was the first and only race I took my mother and father to. Right in front of us was this crash and I don't think they ever wanted to go to a race again.

'It was quite an amazing crash. Jody came round and actually hit the pit wall. Revson went round the back of him and just clipped the rear wing. Jody's car was spun through 360° in a nanosecond. The only damage to Revvie's car was that one of the steering arms was slightly bent. We were able to change that quite quickly and get on with the job. Surtees wasn't happy because it took out the whole of his team.'

John Surtees:

'We were a team that had been set up on a shoestring, but we were developing nicely and becoming competitive. We lost the use of all three cars; they had made different starts and were all involved in the accident. It was a moment when I was seeing before my very eyes my team virtually being wiped out. Jody had attempted to win the race on the first lap. He was a bit impetuous, but if you don't have a go you won't ever do anything. As a pure racer I now understand it to a degree. At the same time, it wasn't sensible. Perhaps the nicest thing that came out of it was that I had some kids send me their pocket money in order to help me get my team back together. That is the memory that I would prefer to keep.'

OPPOSITE TOP: Start of the 1973 British Grand Prix, with Denny Hulme, and eventual winner Peter Revson to the right in the picture. *(Ford)*

OPPOSITE MIDDLE: The end of the first lap and Jody Scheckter is on the grass. Hulme is next round but will avoid him. *(LAT)*

OPPOSITE BOTTOM: Scheckter is now broadside to the track, but Hulme and Revson are away safely. *(LAT)*

LEFT: The morning after. Leo Wybrott took detailed photos of the remains of Scheckter's car. *(Leo Wybrott, courtesy of Jody Scheckter)*

Scheckter led for the first 41 laps of what was only his second Grand Prix and his first with an M23, until Emerson Fittipaldi tried to overtake him in his Lotus 72 and the pair collided. 'Emerson said some things about me after that!'

'I always tried to run less wing on the M23 than anyone else, so I could be quicker on the straights.

'At the British Grand Prix I was behind Denny and Revson on the grid. I must have passed Peter and was right behind Denny. He led me going through Woodcote. I had been running soft tyres in practice, which weren't lasting, so I had brand new, harder tyres that I had not run with before for the race. The car just twitched on me. I went into the pit wall and then bounced back out. I looked up and there were cars crashing before me; I was very lucky not to get hurt. Before the restart I asked where the spare car was, but Phil Kerr just told me to hide away.

'I bought my M23 about ten years ago as is. It is now sitting in a garage in my house, although my son Thomas ran it at the CarFest. I'm a farmer now trying to make this business work.'

David Hobbs

'I had driven McLaren Formula 5000 and Can-Am cars in North America,' recalled David Hobbs. 'I had also driven the Penske McLaren M19 at Watkins Glen in 1971, standing in for Mark Donohue, who chose to race at Trenton that weekend. He did not make up his mind until the Saturday morning so the car was set up for him, which was very different at the rear to how I would have wanted it.

'Having been sponsored in 1973 by Carling Black Label, I was able to take the money to McLaren for a factory drive in the 1974 Indianapolis 500. I had, anyway, known Teddy [Mayer] and Tyler [Alexander] for what seemed like forever.

'Later that year, poor old Mike [Hailwood] broke his legs at the Nürburgring. We were very "pally", as we had driven together a lot in sports car racing and I became a frequent visitor at the hospital. We decided between us that I should drive his McLaren M23. I went on holiday with the family and negotiated with Teddy from a phone box in Sheringham, Norfolk.

BELOW: A young Jody Scheckter in illustrious company at Paul Ricard in 1973. Front row (left to right): Jackie Oliver, Ronnie Peterson, Arturio Merzario, Jackie Stewart. Middle row: Carlos Reutemann, Jean-Pierre Jarier, Scheckter. Back: Emerson Fittipaldi. *(Ford)*

'There was no pre-race testing then, so I went straight to the Österreichring for the Austrian Grand Prix. I had never been there before, so I took time to get up to speed. Phil Kerr was put in charge of my car and we had some significant differences over the set-up. I should have told Phil what I wanted. I realise now that you've got to be firm. I reckon if I had had more say over the set-up I would have gone faster. I was used to more downforce. We had no technical data back then. We both had gut feelings, but I was the one driving the car! Henri Pescarolo was also hanging around the pit with his helmet. He was told to buzz off, but it was rather unsettling.

'I had driven at Monza lots of times, so I knew what I wanted when we went there. I should have demanded more say in the set-up. If I had done better, then I could have kept the drive for the next two races at Mosport and Watkins Glen – tracks I knew very well. Then I might have driven for McLaren the next year. As it was, Jochen Mass got the drive and he stayed with them a long time.

'Forty years ago is a long time, but I seem to remember that the M23 was an easy car to drive and needed only a small amount of fettling.'

Tony Trimmer

'It was the easiest Grand Prix car that I have ever driven,' said Tony Trimmer, who was the last person to score a podium place at an international race with an M23. 'It suited my style, it did everything you asked of it, it put the power down well, it had very neutral handling, it rode the bumps well. It had level tyre wear right through the life of the tyres. It was easy to work on, easy to change the handling – a very small adjustment was easily noticeable. It was a doddle to set the camber. I can't

ABOVE: David Hobbs, seen here at Monza, took over Mike Hailwood's drive for couple of races following his friend's crash at the Nürburgring. *(Ford)*

BELOW: Tony Trimmer in an Aurora round at Oulton Park. *(Jeff Bloxham)*

speak highly enough about it. In particular, it loved Oulton Park and the Grand Prix circuit at Brands Hatch. It was a big wide car, so its aerodynamics were perhaps not so good for Silverstone or Thruxton.

'From the very first race I knew that we were going to win the [Aurora British Formula 1] championship with this car.'

Trimmer, who had once raced a factory Lotus 72 in a non-championship race, went on to try and qualify the fragile, Japanese-built Maki for Grands Prix. Later testing for various Formula 1 teams meant that he drove over 20 different Grand Prix cars. The 72 and the M23 are the two that stand out. 'The M23 had a totally different feel from the Lotus 72. If I had the choice I would go for the M23, but that is not to denigrate the 72. Emerson was so lucky to have raced the two best cars of that era.'

John McCormack

John McCormack was another who drove an M23 in the 1970s, albeit a very different animal – the car he converted to Formula 5000 specification. 'It was much more precise than the Elfin I had driven before. It was a particularly good high-speed car at tracks like Phillip Island. It responded well to aerodynamic adjustment. I put some polypropylene skirts on it, but you had to be doing over 100mph to feel the benefit.

'There was not much feedback on the slower tracks because of the fixed link driveshafts at the back. It did not give you any warning when the back was about to let go. It would hang on and hang on, but when it went, it went. However, I only lost it once when I had new tyres that had not been bedded in.'

RIGHT: John McCormack's conversion of his M23, seen here in second place at Sandown Park, saw it racing against purpose-built Formula 5000s such as this Lola. (LAT)

RIGHT: Yes, it is a McLaren M23. McCormack fitted this bodywork to go Can-Am racing in North America. (Mark Windecker)

THE ROAD TEST THAT NEVER WAS

'Teddy Mayer had never heard of me,' but he had heard of *Motor* magazine,' recalled Gordon Bruce. The former *Motor* road test editor must be the only person to have phoned McLaren out of the blue to ask if he could drive a McLaren M23 and be told that there would be no problem.

James Hunt had just won the World Championship and *Motor* had the not unreasonable idea to run a 'road test' of his McLaren M23. Bruce, who also raced saloons, seemed the ideal staff man for the job, even if his single-seater competition experience had been limited to hill-climbing a 500cc Formula 3 Cooper.

He duly turned up at Silverstone for a seat fitting and a couple of exploratory laps. 'They were very nice to me,' he remembered. 'I vividly recall standing next to James, who was much bigger than me, and then being surprised how difficult it was to get in and out of the car. I felt I was really squeezing myself in.' During his two shake-down laps he also found the M23 was actually quite easy to drive. He was told that the team would be in touch to organise the 'test' proper.

However, the story was not to be. There was confusion at the start of the next season as to when the first round of the World Championship would actually be. 'There was much toing and froing,' said Bruce. The team was unable to commit itself to the test, as it had to rush off to South America. A dummy cover of *Motor* showing the M23 still exists, but it is for the road test that never was.

ABOVE: James Hunt (left) was somewhat larger than Bruce, but the *Motor* road test editor still found difficulty in getting into the M23's cockpit. The article never happened but a dummy cover was made ready. *(Gordon Bruce collection)*

RIGHT: Gordon Bruce, seen here at Prescott in David Latham's Cooper-Norton MkX, was a winner when it came to hillclimbing 500cc Formula 3 cars. However, apart from a track test in a Formula Ford, this was his only single-seater experience before getting in to the M23. *(Author)*

'We seemed to spend an enormous amount of time away from home.'

David Luff
McLaren mechanic 1972–1976

(Ford)

Chapter Four

The mechanic's view

The McLaren M23 was a straightforward, simple car to work on, with everything easily accessible. The mechanics who were employed on it were a tight-knit bunch, most of them seeming to speak with New Zealand accents. Many of them have kept in touch to this day, and at least two of them found themselves working on an M23 as late as 2012.

By the time the McLaren M23 was introduced, Alastair Caldwell had risen from mechanic to team manager, although he was still, effectively, chief mechanic. David Luff took over the post in 1974 until 1976 when a number of changes were made to the team, with Ray Grant looking after James Hunt's car for his championship year. Luff took on a workshop role and Howard Moore became chief mechanic.

Under them was a small band, a number of whom can still be found working in motor sport. Indeed, 'truckie' Roy Reader is still employed by McLaren, although the word 'truckie' has been replaced by 'logistics' and he has been responsible for a whole fleet of trucks where once there was just one.

Mark Scott recalled that McLaren liked to employ young lads, who had the right work ethic and the basic skills, and teach them the McLaren way of doing things. The average number in the crew in 1976, the last full year for the M23, was about 22 or 23. It was a time when each car would have just a couple of mechanics working under the chief mechanic. McLaren normally entered two M23s, except during the year of the splinter, Yardley-sponsored, operation that necessitated a separate team of mechanics under Leo Wybrott.

Alastair Caldwell

There was still a strong Kiwi flavour to the McLaren team in the 1970s. Alastair Caldwell, team manager during the time of the M23, observed that 'the people who would work hard and long hours without complaint were often the colonials'.

Caldwell had worked as an amateur mechanic in New Zealand, one of the first cars being the Lotus 11 of Howden Ganley, and then his brother's Lola. (He had been to school with Ganley, who went on to become a mechanic at McLaren and then a Grand Prix driver in his own right.) He decided to go to England in 1967 and 'have a go at professional motor racing for "a short period". I arrived with no knowledge of the geography of the country, but I had an aunt who lived in Gerrards Cross so she picked me up from the airport and

BELOW: **The winners. Celebrating their 1974 World Championship are (left to right) David Luff, Howard Moore, Phil Sharp and Tyler Alexander with Gordon Coppuck on the Armco.** *(David Luff collection)*

McLAREN M23 FACTORY MECHANICS 1973–77

Kerry Adams
Gary Anderson
Steve Bunn
Alastair Caldwell
Graham Cook
Ray Grant
John Hornby
Salvatore Incandella
David Luff
Howard Moore
Dave Ryan

Mike Sales
Mark Scott
Phil Sharp
Kevin Stone
Barry Sullivan
Cary Taylor
Leo Wybrott

Truckies
Roy Reader
Lance Gibbs

LEFT: Hardly ideal working conditions. Monaco in the wet. *(David Luff collection)*

LEFT: The 1976 winning team with James Hunt. (Left to right) Roy Reader, Howard Moore, Ray Grant, Lance Gibbs, Alastair Caldwell, Gordon Coppuck and Teddy Mayer. *(Alastair Caldwell collection)*

took me to her house. I said I would like to visit McLaren's and she said that was no problem as it was just down the road in Colnbrook. She took me there the next morning; I asked for a job and they took me on as a cleaner.'

That evening when he should have gone home, Caldwell started to help the mechanics, and at 2 o'clock next morning Tyler Alexander, then the chief mechanic, said it was time to go home. Alexander started again at 7am so Caldwell was sitting on the doorstep at 6.45am. Alexander let him in and gave him some work to do on one of the cars. 'So my career as a cleaner lasted only eight hours!'

By the 1967 Italian Grand Prix, Caldwell was deputed to take the truck to Monza. Before long he was number one mechanic on Bruce's car, then chief mechanic and, in 1972, team manager.

'The Can-Am and IndyCar teams were so successful that the Formula 1 team was almost an orphan, and its success almost came as a surprise,' recalled Caldwell. 'I prided myself that the cars were always the most reliable. Bits did not fall off them, and that was the reason we got Fittipaldi. Our cars were always overweight. It was not until I went to Brabham that I realised you could make a car underweight! I didn't want any fancy materials on my cars. The ethos at McLaren was reliability. Everything else was subject to that. We didn't put innovative stuff on the car until it had been proven.

'I got to be team manager. We did OK in 1973 but didn't really get the results. In 1974 we had a horrendous time because all three drivers had contracts that said they had to have cars the same. Hulme and Hailwood had to have the same as Fittipaldi. Hailwood had to have two cars and the Marlboro Texaco team had to have three.

'Fittipaldi was an inveterate fiddler, and we never raced the car in the same configuration. That year the M23 was never the same at any race. It was shorter, longer, wider. There were so many spacers – 6in, 12in. Did we ring the changes? We had to do it for all five cars! That year was a nightmare from a logistics point of view. Fittipaldi was a good test driver but perhaps a little too enthusiastic for new bits. Including Can-Am IndyCar, Formula 2 and Formula 5000, we built and ran nine cars that year and we won in every category. We didn't make the bodywork – that was done by Specialised Moulding – but the monocoque, the suspension, the uprights, everything else we made. We even painted the cars. We had just 34 employees, and that included two tea ladies.

'We used to be "on it" from the first race – none of this "we'll get better as the season goes on". The points for the first race count just as much as for the last. That first one can be easier to win as the competition may still be warming itself up. In those days, Grand Prix racing was almost amateur.

'One of my jobs was to interpret the rules. One of the reasons why McLaren was so successful was that I used to sit and read the rules, and decide what they said, as opposed to what everybody thought they said. It's only what lawyers do.'

David Luff

David Luff, better known as 'Luffy', was McLaren's chief mechanic for a major period in the life of the M23. 'I had been working with Brabham since about 1964. In 1970 I left to go on a round the world trip. When I came back, Alastair [Caldwell] asked if I would join McLaren as a mechanic for Peter Revson. Two of us worked on his M19, a New Zealander Phil Sharp and myself. When the M23 came to life, Phil and I stayed working on the car and we won the British Grand Prix. We seemed to spend an enormous amount of time in other countries, because the only place that you could test was somewhere that was hot. We would find we were away for weeks and weeks, and then we would come back and start the season, and off we went again.

'We got to Watkins Glen and we were trying lots of different tyre configurations, including some that would have looked more at home on a dragster. We had these things that Goodyear

LEFT: 'Luffy' in 1973. The hat wasn't obligatory team wear. *(David Luff collection)*

BELOW: David Luff appears to be eyeing 'Revie's' champagne after the 1973 British Grand Prix. *(David Luff collection)*

ABOVE: David Luff
rummages in an M23's
sidepod at the 1973 US
Grand Prix. (David Luff
collection)

called O1s, and there was only one set per
team. Although I was mechanic on Revie's car
I was leaning towards engineering more than
anything else. Revie would come in and ask,
"Where's my tyres?" How was I going to explain
that Teddy [Mayer] had given them to Jody
[Scheckter] to try. "Jesus Christ, the kid's got
my tyres," said Revie. He was out of the car;
I'd never seen him blow up like that. He went
ballistic at Teddy.

'I had great admiration for Revie. He was an
absolute gentleman. He wanted me to go with
him to Shadow, but I had only just bought my
first house in Windsor.

BELOW: David Luff's
armband from Monaco
in 1973. (David Luff
collection)

'At the end of the year we went back to
Paul Ricard testing, with Denny trying things
like different noses. Then Emerson came along
to test there. It was a dreadful day, with typical
Paul Ricard mistral wind. At the end of a full
day's test, Emerson spun the car. When he
came back he said, "David, I don't know what
happened, I never spin." I said he must have
been caught by the high wind, but he was
quite bemused.

'By this time I was called "chief mechanic".
Whilst still working on Emerson's car, I had
more of an overseeing role. Phil Sharp
continued working on that car along with
Kevin Stone. Everything moved around at that
point, and Alastair assumed the role of team
manager, which took him out of the mainstream
mechanical side.

'The 1974 season was an unbelievable
experience. I was working with somebody
who I knew could win not only races but also
championships. It became very clear with
Emerson, right from the beginning, that we
were up for a serious challenge. Emerson,
himself, was a great guy. Again, a gentleman

who would always say "good morning" to every mechanic in the pits. When we went to Brazil we were treated like heroes. Because Marlboro sponsored us there were parties wherever we went. We were one family, not a big one because there were still just two mechanics on each car, plus myself as a floater and Roy Reader as the tyre engineer. Add Alastair, Teddy and Gordon and the few guys back in the workshop, and that was it.

'1975 was a bit of a strange year. We didn't follow up winning the World Championship as we might have done, and things like Jochen Mass crashing three times at the Nürburgring were difficult to recover from.

'It was always a difficult car to get into first gear. Whenever we changed an engine, one of the first things we did was to bleed the air out of the clutch. You could not sit on the grid for long with the car in gear, so the drivers would take them out and then at about the 30-second board try to select the right gear. You could not just push the gearlever over to the left and then hook it back because it would not go in. You had to wait a nanosecond and then let

the engine revs come down a bit as you were selecting it. At one race, Emerson could not find the gear and he was still trying to get started when Denny hit the back of the car enough to make it turn the gearbox. It selected the gear and off they went. However, Emerson's car was too badly damaged.

'At Monza once, Jochen got as far as the first chicane before having a contretemps with somebody else, being launched into the air and landing on his right front. That bent the front rocker, and he immediately came back into the pits. There were no radios in those days, so we had no advance warning and there was a big panic from the wall. Alastair had a talk with the driver and it was only then that we realised the front rocker was slightly bent. We tried to screw the shock absorber adjuster up to compensate for the amount that it was bent. He did a couple more laps. In today's world the car would have been retired then and there.

'I can also remember Denny coming in with his seatbelts undone. The finger was pointed at the mechanic, but as he was driving Denny had swung his arms around in the confined area of

BELOW: More pressure for the McLaren mechanics. A pit-stop race at Silverstone. *(David Luff collection)*

the cockpit and knocked the buckle.

'Bizarrely, that year we had one or two plug leads come off, and so the car would come in with a misfire. When the DFV was first built it would have a little rubber cover popped in the hole to stop any dirt ingress. Now we had moved on to specially moulded silicone plugs that were quite hard to push in. When it popped out we would put the plug lead back in again, but then five or six laps later it would pop out again. I think we had two or three incidents like this. Finally we worked out what was going wrong. The chamber where the plug screwed into the head was hollow all the way through. The plug part of the head was water-cooled and it had to have a perfect seal when pressed into the head. We found that tiny droplets of water had made their way out of that seal. Because we had used these moulded plugs we had effectively made a kettle. There was nowhere for the steam to go and the pressure would build up, so out would come the plug taking the lead with it. It took us quite a while to understand this. We found there was a bolt screwed into the back of the cam cover into which we just drilled a tiny 1/16 in hole. This meant that it could never be a kettle again as the steam would be able to come out of this hole. We came across all sorts of little problems like that.

'At Brazil we were running pretty competitively until Hailwood crashed the car

LEFT: **A McLaren
factory scene, with
David Luff in the
foreground.** (David
Luff collection)

of the splinter team. We knew of no reason
why this should have happened, except we
thought the lower rear wishbone had broken.
We had to strengthen this up for the race. This
was an unbelievable situation. We had to cut
a piece of something like an inch round tube
lengthways down the centre and then weld
this half round cap on to the original wishbone.
Brazil was a pretty dreadful place to work. We
were all in this whopping great big wooden
shed. However, Alastair and myself set about
strengthening these wishbones. That night there
was a massive electrical thunderstorm and we
continued gas welding standing on race tyres;
we could see lightning bolts hitting the ground
on the other side of the track. Alan McCall, who
had been at McLaren but was now working for
the Hexagon team, came along with a bottle

of brandy to give us encouragement. It was a
bizarre evening, but one I remember vividly. The
cars were now reliable and we finished the race.

'1975 was rather a lacklustre year and
we did not know whether Emerson had any
intentions of leaving. But he may have known
that he might be going to his brother's team. It
did not seem the same as the previous years.
In 1976 I stopped going with the teams and
mainly stayed in the workshop, I didn't feel that
I wanted to go racing at that time.

'The M23 was in general a very simple
car to work on, very easy. You could get at
everything; it was very accessible. You could
take the gearbox off in ten minutes. Compared
to the Lotus 80 that I am working on now, it
was a joy. You could overcome virtually any
eventuality in a very short space of time.'

'Luffy' also recalled how the evolution of the suspension resulted in a new nickname for himself and Alastair Caldwell. 'The rear suspension started life as a tubular structure that bolted through two ears on the top of the gearbox. With the loads going in, it had to have a triangulation frame made to join up to where the top damper unit went. Alastair and I ended up getting the nickname of "Hack and Slash, the beam stay men". The structure on the top of the box was called the beam. Back then everything was made out of tube welded with argon, never with the exactness of today. One side might be up a little bit, the other down. So Alastair and I ended up making beam stays for each individual top beam. Over the years, Gordon Coppuck would come up with different geometries – maybe the tyre diameter would change – so we were constantly making different beam stays. A progression was the one we made in aluminium. We started to understand that machining parts on a mill was far more accurate than lifting and bending and trying to get points where we thought they

should be. The aluminium one was given the name "The Firth of Forth Bridge". It was two aluminium plates that had been made on a mill, so had accurate holes. Then there was a plate to make it like a half H section, and that was drilled and tapped and screwed on to these two individual plates. There were constant evolution changes, but none of them was ever difficult to make.'

Leo Wybrott

Leo Wybrott joined McLaren in 1970 as project engineer. It was an idea that he had had at Lotus. Rather than the mechanics being responsible for building the cars as well as racing them, a team of ex-mechanics, or people with an engineering background, should build the cars in the workshop, take them initially to a test and then hand them over to the team. This started with the M14 and continued with the M19. By the time the M23 was introduced there was an established team working under

BELOW: The mechanics with Jochen Mass at Silverstone in 1975. (Ford)

DON BERESFORD

In the 1970s, the design department and car build at McLaren worked much more closely to create the finished product than today. There were fewer designers with far less time and facilities compared to now, when pretty much every small detail is handled by design and then enacted by car build. In those days, people like Gordon Coppuck relied on others such as Leo Wybrott, Alastair Caldwell and the late Don Beresford to fill in a lot of gaps.

Beresford joined McLaren in 1965, just as it began its Formula 1 design and build programme, immediately becoming involved in the car build process. In 1967 and 1968 he combined this with work as chief mechanic on Denny Hulme's Can-Am cars. He subsequently became factory based, working as works foreman with responsibility for liaison with the design office, planning and execution of the car build programmes, and management of the factory's production personnel and activities, including giving opportunities to the many hopefuls from the Antipodes who turned up on the doorstep at Colnbrook.

While the draughtsmen were pushing ahead with component design and general layout, Beresford would map out a working plan for the 12 weeks that it would take his team to finish a car after receiving the first drawings. Writing in a McLaren brochure at the time of the M19 (the M23's predecessor) Beresford said: 'The monocoques we build now are really sophisticated. They bear no resemblance to the monocoques we were making… five years ago when I joined the team. We have learned how to use aluminium panels to best advantage, and by working with Reynolds Aluminium engineers we now change gauges of sheet in various parts of the tub. For safety reasons we are skinning the outside of the chassis with 16 gauge aluminium.'

Beresford was later responsible for the development of McLaren's capability using composite materials – initially with aluminium-skinned/honeycomb-cored structures, and subsequently with carbon composites.

ABOVE: Don Beresford demonstrates the M23's fuelling coupler. *(Nigel Beresford collection)*

Wybrott. Equally involved was Don Beresford, who was in overall charge of the workshop. Wybrott would pick up the work with the design staff from the early concept, while the chassis would be built under Beresford's guidance. 'Whilst this was happening, I would be working on the suspension and other components of the car, so that when the chassis was finished we would be able to integrate them.' Wybrott was, by now, project manager and the pair had their individual roles.

Not long after the first car, a couple more M23s were laid down. 'Once we had one built we could then produce more parts at a much quicker rate in readiness for the tub.

'I oversaw and helped to build all of the

RIGHT: Pushing Revson to the start at Silverstone 1973.
(David Luff collection)

BELOW: Kerry Adams' notes from the 1975 Race of Champions.

Track BRANDS HATCH Event Race of Champs Driver MASS
Date 16.3.75 Temp. Mech.
Chassis No. M23·8 Engine No. 061

Gears: 12·38 1st 15·53 2nd 16·30 3rd 18·29 4th 19·28 5th
RPM Pulled   Fuel Setting 076 ON 4½
Oil Press.   Oil Temp.   Water Temp.
Ign. Setting   Boost

F. Rim   F. Tyre   F. Press
R. Rim   R. Tyre   R. Press

F. Roll Bar ·275	·422		R. Roll Bar ·023 x 7 ·945			
F. Shocks SHORT	SP4		R. Shocks SP4			
F. Spring 275			R. Spring RVA			
F. Toe-In ·10° OUT			R. Toe-In SET 55			
F. Castor 3			R. Castor			
F. Wing GO?? /	DELTA		R. Wing MID - ?? ?			

(With Driver & ½ Fuel Load)

F. Ride Ht. 2½   R. Ride Ht. 3½
L.F. Camber 3/8N R.F. Camber 7/8N L.R. Camber ½N R.R. Camber ¼N
L.F. Weight   R.F. Weight   L.R. Weight   R.R. Weight

Fuel Start   Miles Per Lap
Fuel Add.   Laps Completed
Total In   Total Miles
Fuel Out
Fuel Used   Fuel Consump.

Misc. Data

Driver Requests :

M23 chassis. I also built to a high show specification, and delivered the Marlboro show cars. The show cars were Marlboro property so we never saw them back again.'

The introduction of the separate Yardley team, which was run by Phil Kerr, gave Wybrott new responsibilities. He travelled to the early races that season with Kerry Adams and John Hornby. From the Silverstone International Trophy onwards, the Yardley team had two cars to use, M23/1 and M23/7, both of which were crashed by Hailwood at the Nürburgring. Although the Yardley team continued for the rest of the season, Wybrott was no longer involved with it.

Kerry Adams

It would be Kerry Adams's second time at McLaren when he accepted an approach from Alastair Caldwell for the 1974 season, because back in late 1970 he had been loaned to the team by Frank Williams. 'It was a bit bemusing. When I first came over in 1969, McLaren wouldn't give me a job,' recalled Adams, another New Zealander.

'I started with Leo Wybrott on Mike Hailwood's Yardley car, but it was not long before Alastair wanted me on the Marlboro team. I looked after the spare car that year. There was only me looking after it. We didn't have the capacity for two spare cars and it was primarily set up for Emerson. For 1975 I was put in charge of Jochen Mass's car. I was asked whom I would like as my mechanic. I had seen this lad, Dave Ryan, sweeping the floor, and thought he had potential so I asked for him.' (Ryan was to remain with McLaren for over three decades, eventually becoming Sporting Director.)

'I left at the beginning of 1976, but then I got a call from Teddy [Mayer] to come back and work in the shop. That meant working on the M24 and M26, but also still the M23 as we struggled to keep it competitive. I had my off-road Kawasaki motorcycle in bits at the time, and that was the inspiration for the six-speed box. However, it was Alastair's idea; you've got to give him credit for that. I left at the end of

the year to work in the Can-Am Challenge with Chris Amon.'

Adams was not, though, finished with the M23. At the end of 1978 he set up in business with designer Alan McCall, buying his partner out three years later. In his new role he was to work on rebuilding or preparing four M23s, starting by restoring M23/8-2 for Albert Obrist. As a result of this, he carried out the same task for Ernst Schuster when he acquired M23/11. The M23 that today sits in McLaren's lobby was also restored by Adams, one of five cars that he has done for the company.

Adams's business is now located on Jody Scheckter's premises, and one of his tasks is to look after the South African's collection of cars – the story of how he acquired M23/2 being told elsewhere in this book. When the car was rolled out at the 2012 CarFest, Adams was abroad, so he employed former colleague David Luff to look after the car that day.

BELOW: M23/2 outside Kerry Adams's workshop. With Adams abroad at the time, David Luff prepared the car for the 2012 CarFest at Laverstoke Park. *(David Luff)*

John Hornby

John Hornby had been working at Ferrari importer Maranello Concessionaires before joining McLaren at the end of 1972. He recalled: 'When I was shown round the workshop the front bulkhead and the rear bulkhead of the first M23 were on the jig. By the time I started with the build team the tub was coming off the jig. I went to one or two races during 1973. Then the Marlboro–Yardley clash happened and McLaren had to run a third car, so I ended up working with Kerry Adams and Leo Wybrott on the Mike Hailwood car; a very enjoyable time it was. We had to be quite separate at the circuit from the Philip Morris side. We only had one car, so we could finish our work before them!

'At the end of 1974, McLaren decided to have a specialist gearbox man, so we built the "Hewland Arms". The stores were revamped, and space under the mezzanine floor was used to make two rooms, one an office for Don Beresford, the other a workshop for myself to do the gearboxes. Lance Gibbs, who was with us then, was a very good signwriter, and I

persuaded him to do signs for above the doors; mine was "The Hewland Arms" and Don's was "The Steering Wheel Club".'

In addition to the six-speed gearbox, Hornby also had a hand in another of the M23's innovations. 'I was quite involved in getting the air starter on the car. The fuel pump was right at the bottom of the tank and on the side of the DFV, and Alastair [Caldwell] and Gordon [Coppuck] wanted to move it. They spent a long time trying to work out how they could transfer it from the bottom left-hand corner of the engine to the top right-hand cam box to drive it off the end of the camshaft. There was very little clearance between the end of the DFV and the back of the tub on that side. It got to lunchtime and I wandered past, sandwich in hand, as they had the fuel pump in a million bits, measuring it all up. I said that rev counter drive on the left-hand side camshaft is only about an inch wide. That would go on the right-hand side. Why not move it and then put the fuel pump in the big gap left? Gordon immediately realised how obvious it was.'

Hornby, appropriately known as 'Dublo', stayed working on gearboxes until he left McLaren in 1979. He briefly returned to McLaren International in the 1980s, but then continued his association with Teddy Mayer by joining his CART team, Mayer Motor Racing, in the USA. He stayed with the American when he teamed up with Carl Haas and returned to Formula 1 with the Lola-built Beatrices. This was followed by a long association with Xtrac founder Mike Endean, which continues to this day.

Hornby has more than just memories of the McLaren M23. He not only owns the contorted steering wheel off the car that Mike Hailwood crashed at Monte Carlo's Casino Square, he also has the very steering wheel that was in James Hunt's car the day he clinched the world title in Fuji. 'Other people claim they have the steering wheel off Hunt's car from Japan, but I know I have. I didn't go to the pub that day, while most people did, and I swapped the steering wheel over,' he said.

Mark Scott

Although born in the UK, Mark Scott had been brought up in New Zealand, so was another who added to the Kiwi flavour of the early McLaren set-up. There being no openings in the race team, he had begun working with the Nicholson McLaren engine operation in 1975, mainly on Cosworth DFVs for Embassy Hill until the tragic aircraft accident that claimed the lives of Graham Hill and three of his team. At the end of the year there was a change around at McLaren. 'John Steenson, the shop foreman at Nicholson McLaren, another Kiwi, knew that I wanted to work with the race team and so he made a recommendation for me. I had decided by that time that I really did not have the patience to rebuild DFVs; it was just not in my make-up.

'It was winter, and being one of the new lads I went from department to department and helped build a couple of show cars. Work had just started on the M26 and I tended to help out on odd fabrication jobs. At the start of the 1976 season I began work as number two mechanic under Davey Ryan on Jochen Mass's car. The team was quite small then, with only two mechanics per car along with Roy Reader, the truck driver. I think there were only eight workers, plus people like Alastair [Caldwell] and Teddy [Mayer].

'Later in the year, I became number two under Gary Anderson to run the T-car, mainly for Hunt that year. They would move people around just to suit the various personalities. Howard Moore was Hunt's number one mechanic; Ray Grant would work with him as his number two. The rest of us would fill in. The following year,

we ran Villeneuve and Giacomelli. It turned out there were some interesting people used that car.

'The M26 came out after the British GP, but it was a bit difficult so it went back to the factory, and Hughie Absalom was charged with the task of making it a winner. We went back to the M23 until he had sorted it out. I much preferred working on the M23 to the M26. They were two totally different cars, and some of that was because the M23 was well sorted by the time I got to work on it. It was a very simple car, especially by today's standards. It took just two of us to rebuild it.

'There were a couple of things that were a pain in the butt. For instance, the engine had to come out to enable us to change the radiators. If you weren't too careful drilling and riveting in the Lexan skirts underneath the car, you could puncture the radiator. Then you had to pull out the whole engine to get the radiator out. The complicated outer ball joints of the front suspension were another idiosyncrasy. It was a spherical bearing that was specially ground with tiny ball bearings in it, top and bottom, to allow it to turn easily. Emerson had earlier complained that the suspension was too heavy. Otherwise, the car was quite simple and easy to maintain.

'Most of us were quite young on the team; we were all in our early twenties. Alastair Caldwell was the most experienced person on the team, and the rest of us had not been there long. Alastair was quite a strong leader. Another strong leader was Roy Reader, the truck driver. He had been around for a long, long time and probably knew more about the cars than half the mechanics. He was one of the 'go-to' people on the team. At one point, when we had no chief mechanic, the crew tried to get him elected. It did not matter what happened to the race car, he always had the part you needed on the truck, and Roy always knew where it was. We were quite spoilt to have someone of that calibre as a truck driver... and he is still there today.'

Scott retains fond memories of the 1976 season. 'At the beginning of the year we started putting front roll hoops on the car, and put a cap on the rear roll hoop for James. He was concerned about being able to get out of the car if it was upside down. We turned a car upside down in the workshop with him in it to see if he could bust his way out through the side bodywork.

'It was obviously going to be very hot in Argentina. There were no drinks systems then, and Alastair decided we should put a Thermos in the nose box and run some lines back into the cockpit and under the driver's balaclava. On the way back to the hotel one night we stopped off at a supermarket. Alastair made sure that nobody was looking and then dropped the various Thermoses on display to see which one did not shatter. We found one that seemed to hold up for a couple of drops, so put that back and got a new one. We strapped this to the inside of the nose box on Hunt's car for the race. James started the race, accelerated away, and all the orange juice came surging backwards up the tube, which was not in his mouth at the time, and filled his helmet.

'There was a great thrash at the British Grand Prix when they had that first lap crash. That was a tremendous experience. We brought the T-car out, put it on the grid and then raced back to the garage with the race car to try to fix it. We did it while Denny Hulme stood on Hunt's spot on the grid making sure that the race would not start again without him. James then 'won' the race. They used then to have that wonderful tradition of putting the race car up on a flat-bed truck and then driving it all the way round the track. The whole crew got up there, and by the time we had completed the lap we were all completely drunk because we had been consuming champagne the whole way round.'

The result of that race may have been overturned but, said Scott, 'We know we won it!'

'The Japanese Grand Prix that year was another classic, with that mysterious occasion between James and Teddy as to whether he should come in and get fresh tyres. Luckily for us, when he had two tyres go down he was approaching the pit entry and was able to make it into the pits. Then James did not know if he had won the championship. It had been such an up and down year for us. We went into those last three races with only a mathematical chance of winning it, so it was fantastic to realise that long shot.'

Gary Anderson

Formula 1 designer and BBC technical analyst, Gary Anderson, joined McLaren for the final year of the M23. 'It was getting long in the tooth by then, having been around for five years. Any car that old needs bringing back to life. It was a good mechanical car. We ran it very stiff to try to get it to work with the tyres. It was before the days when we understood aerodynamics, so there was nothing we could do about that.' Anderson was deputed to assist with the development of the then unloved and temporarily retired M26, but still carried out duties on the spare, getting it ready for the next race. 'I worked all hours and sundry.'

Roy Reader

Roy Reader joined McLaren in March 1972 as a 'transport driver cum spares man' and is still there today having headed the logistics side of what has become a vastly different business. Within a week he was employed at the Race of Champions, driving a left-hand-drive panel van between the old sloping paddock on the outside of Brands Hatch, the pits and the factory at Colnbrook. 'It wasn't a very good opener!'

'In the early days I was a "jack-of-all-trades" – extra mechanic, fuel man, logistics person, you name it.' Reader initially stayed with the company until 1984, then had six years away before rejoining. 'In 1973 we had one truck (a Ford D600 with Eaton two-speed split gearbox). Now we've got 22!' This remained so during the active life of the M23, with the exception of 1974 when a second truck was used. David Luff reckoned that this might have been the first articulated vehicle to be used in Formula 1.

There was no time limit then on how long a truck driver could remain at the wheel, and much of the time Reader was the sole driver. He would sometimes be assisted by one of the mechanics, such as Barry Sullivan or Howard Moore, or even, on occasion, by team manager Alastair Caldwell who, he recalled, held a New Zealand heavy goods vehicle licence.

Despite the distances covered and the hours worked, there was only one serious

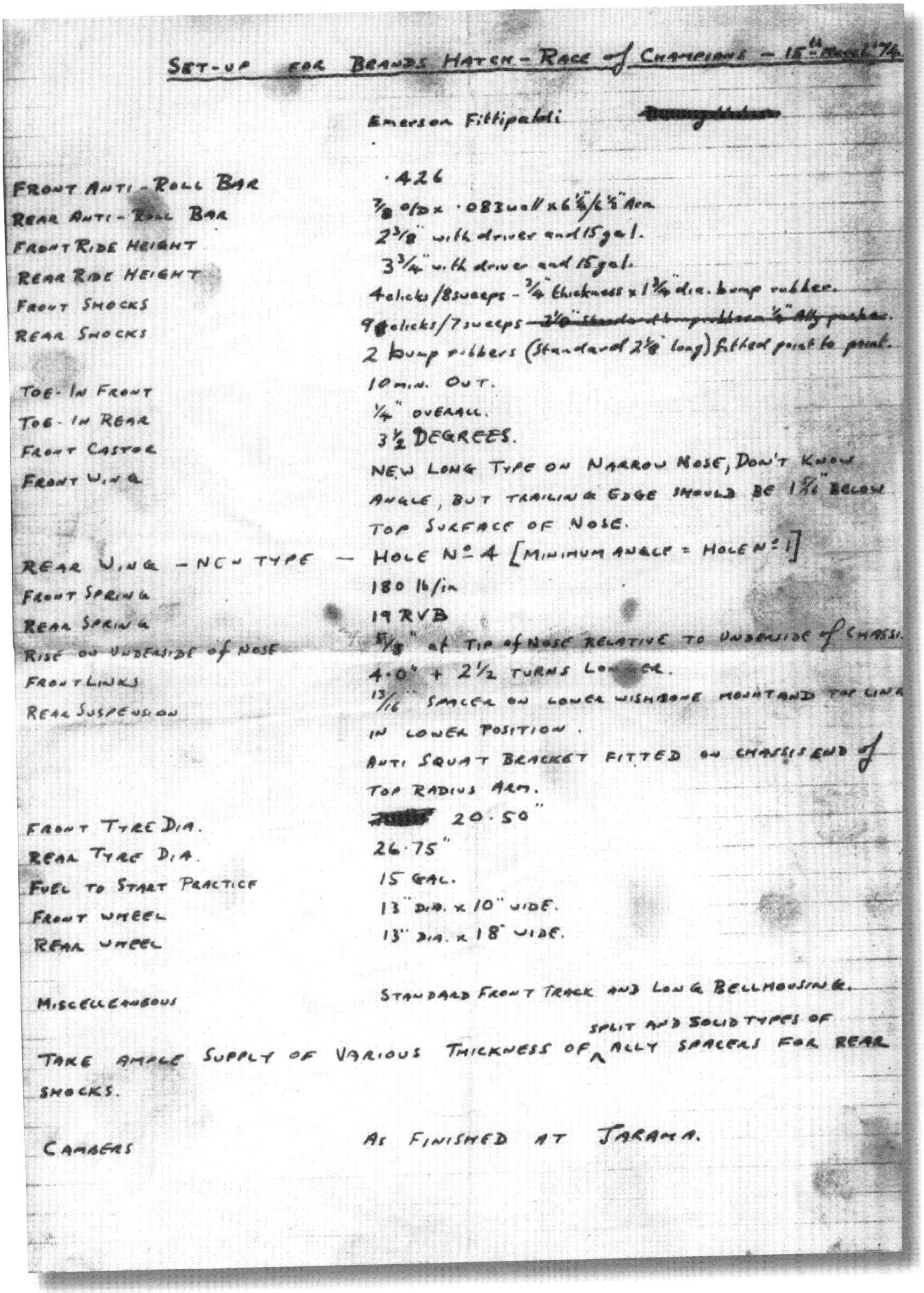

SET-UP FOR BRANDS HATCH – RACE of CHAMPIONS – 15th March 1974.

Emerson Fittipaldi ~~[illegible]~~

FRONT ANTI-ROLL BAR	·426
REAR ANTI-ROLL BAR	7/8 O/D x ·083 wall x 6 1/8"/6 1/8" Arm
FRONT RIDE HEIGHT	2 3/8" with driver and 15 gal.
REAR RIDE HEIGHT	3 3/4" with driver and 15 gal.
FRONT SHOCKS	4 clicks/8 sweeps – 3/4" thickness x 1 3/4" dia. bump rubber.
REAR SHOCKS	9 clicks/7 sweeps ~~2 1/2" Standard bump rubber 1/2" Ally [illegible]~~
	2 bump rubbers (Standard 2 1/8" long) fitted point to point.
TOE-IN FRONT	10 min. OUT.
TOE-IN REAR	1/4" OVERALL.
FRONT CASTOR	3 1/2 DEGREES.
FRONT WING	NEW LONG TYPE ON NARROW NOSE, DON'T KNOW ANGLE, BUT TRAILING EDGE SHOULD BE 1 5/16" BELOW TOP SURFACE OF NOSE.
REAR WING – NEW TYPE –	HOLE No 4 [MINIMUM ANGLE = HOLE No 1]
FRONT SPRING	180 lb/in
REAR SPRING	19 RVB
RISE ON UNDERSIDE of NOSE	5/8" at TIP of NOSE RELATIVE TO UNDERSIDE of CHASSIS
FRONT LINKS	4·0" + 2 1/2 TURNS LONGER.
REAR SUSPENSION	13/16" SPACER ON LOWER WISHBONE MOUNT AND TOP LINK IN LOWER POSITION.
	ANTI SQUAT BRACKET FITTED ON CHASSIS END of TOP RADIUS ARM.
FRONT TYRE DIA.	~~[illegible]~~ 20·50"
REAR TYRE DIA.	26·75"
FUEL TO START PRACTICE	15 GAL.
FRONT WHEEL	13" DIA. x 10" WIDE.
REAR WHEEL	13" DIA. x 18" WIDE.
MISCELLANEOUS	STANDARD FRONT TRACK AND LONG BELLHOUSING.

TAKE AMPLE SUPPLY OF VARIOUS THICKNESS OF SPLIT AND SOLID TYPES OF ALLY SPACERS FOR REAR SHOCKS.

CAMBERS AS FINISHED AT JARAMA.

LEFT: Set-up sheet for the 1974 Race of Champions.

incident during this time, which was when Reader and mechanic Steve Bunn were heading from Spain to testing at the Paul Ricard circuit in France. A couple of young Spaniards, on their way back from a football match, were overtaking on the blind bend of a mountainous road. Reader hit the brakes hard and the artic jack-knifed. Sadly, the car finished up underneath the truck and the lads were killed. The police quickly arrived and, as was the way in Spain, even the judiciary set up by the side of the road. Witnesses testified

an early Williams and
Alastair Caldwell in
Jody Scheckter's M23
on the set of *Rush!*.
(Nichola Aigner)

to Reader's undoubted innocence and the pair would have been allowed on their way apart from the fact that, while the trailer was undamaged, the tractor unit would have to be taken to the docks at Santander on a low loader. A problem arose from the fact that to get through customs in Spain then, the team needed ATA carnets and they were not going to be allowed on the boat until all had been suitably signed. Texaco came to their aid but 'we spent a whole week at Santander,' remembered Reader. Eventually, the tractor unit was fork-lifted on to a boat, which meant more difficulties getting it off at Portsmouth. Reader then had just a week back in England before driving off again to Belgium.

Customs were always a problem in those days, particularly in Spain where Reader would often have to spend a day getting out of the country. Packs of Marlboro stickers or similar 'goodies' could often ease the passage, but it

did not do to follow the truck of another team that gave away jackets and T-shirts, because the officials would expect more than Reader could give. Selling collections of Marlboro stickers in North America also gave the mechanics a few extra cents.

'It was fantastic being able to run the M23 for so many years. It was a dream car for any us to work on, a mechanic-friendly car. Whatever driver you put in an M23 could do something with it. There was also a unique bond in the team that probably came from Bruce; other teams envied our relationships. Everybody would do whatever needed to be done. The drivers such as Emerson, Jochen and James, were also fun guys to be with.'

As a member of the McLaren team that worked with the M23 and who is still employed by the company, Reader reflects on the difference between Grand Prix racing then and now. 'You couldn't work the hours we did then!'

DAVID LUFF NOTES PIT LANE AND PADDOCK CHANGES THAT COULD BE MADE TO A McLAREN M23

■ We would have a basic set-up that Gordon Coppuck would come up with in the factory. It was such a simple car that it did not have anything tricky about it. The only thing was that the front roll bar was a torsion bar, while the rear was the old type of bent tube. That was something of an innovation, using a machined bar that came in various different sizes. One was about $3/8$in diameter, and I think the biggest we ever got up to was just about $9/16$in. We went down to a very small one that was like a knitting needle, which we used for the wet conditions, when you would try to soften up the car. Alastair came up with an innovation as to how you would pull out a pin and then one end of the roll bar arm would become effectively inoperative. That way, if the race conditions went from dry to wet, it would be possible to disconnect the front roll bar in a short space of time.

■ The toes, front and rear, were easily adjusted by an arm coming from the steering rack with a left and right thread. Sometimes Gordon would increase or decrease toe in or out. We generally ran with toe out. Perhaps Emerson would want a bit more bite from the front, and then Gordon would calculate how much would increase or decrease the amount of toe out. It was also very simple to do.

■ Ride heights we tended not to mess with too much. The car would be pretty much how it left the factory, because we became familiar with what attitude the car would like to run at. Therefore, that rake tended to remain pretty much the same.

■ It was always a fairly bulletproof car. There was nothing that you would say was fragile. It always amazed me that Gordon had a $3/8$in-diameter bolt on the outside end of the steering arm, whereas a Lotus might have a $10/32$in, about a third of the McLaren's diameter. One area we did have to keep out eye on and check before the race would be the clutch release bearing. This was a pretty

agricultural thing from a Ford Transit. Quite often the drivers would leave their foot on the clutch rather than on the little stop that we provided on the side of the monocoque. That meant the release bearing would be constantly spinning. Thus we would always fit a new bearing before the race, but that was no big deal as the gearbox could be taken off in less than half an hour. There were four bolts for the radius rods, something like seven bolts and two nuts for the bell housing and the gearbox would be off.

■ The McLaren M23 started with an M19 rear wing, which we ran in South Africa. Then we went on to a double plate arrangement with a massive load of holes. The regulations at that time said that the maximum height of the rear wing and the maximum back offset, measured from the axle centre line to the furthest part of the rear wing, had to be as specified by the FIA. So, we had the holes Gordon had designed that would always keep the rear part of the wing within the legal tolerances. The wings changed. We had huge rear ones for high downforce areas but a much smaller one at Monza. So, there were lots of different plate arrangements. They looked like Swiss cheese because of the number of holes in them. Teddy came up with a number 'N1', which would be the least angle of the rear wing. 'N2' would be more, and so on. I still refer to 'N1' as the least of anything; 'N8' is the most.

■ The biggest thing to change would be the aeons, or bump rubbers, which slid on the shaft of the shock absorbers. When the shock absorber closed to minimum, instead of clashing metal-to-metal it would sit on the bump rubber. Gordon might want to keep the ride height where it was, but the track might be bumpy under braking and the car might have hit the road, so we would have to introduce another piece of bump rubber. This was probably the longest job that we would have to do on an M23.

'The M23s are just great cars.'

Rob Hall
Partner, Hall and Hall

(Jon Bunston)

Chapter Five

Restoration and historic racing

Of the 13 McLaren M23s built, all but one remains in a complete state. McLaren still retains one while, until mid-2012, there were two private owners with two apiece. Fittingly, one is based in New Zealand, four are in the USA, one is owned by a Spaniard, while six are in the UK. Although less so in recent years, a number of these cars have participated in historic racing.

Although it is the newer and usually less important cars from the 1966–85 3-litre Formula 1 era that appear most in historic racing, there is still a place for the McLaren M23. Such cars have appeared in competition on both sides of the Atlantic, while others, like the one now owned by Jody Scheckter, are confined to occasional demonstrations or, like that still owned by McLaren, are mainly static exhibitions. As WDK Motorsport engineer Jonathan Hoad (who was not even born when the M23 competed in Grands Prix) says, 'To be able to work on these cars is quite awe inspiring.'

Buying and maintaining a McLaren M23

Despite their obvious rarity, McLaren M23s still occasionally change hands. For example, Scott Walker sold one of his two, M23/11, to Charles Nearburg in 2012. Amongst those who have bought and sold M23s is the specialist dealer, Duncan Hamilton & Co. Ltd, founded by the 1953 Le Mans winner of that name and now run by his son, Adrian. 'Buying cars,' observes Adrian Hamilton, 'is a very simple process, whether it is a Morris 1100 or a McLaren M23.'

Having made this observation, he does point out an obvious difference. 'The most important thing is the provenance and the history of the car. The condition is totally secondary. Anything can be fixed, but you can't repeat the history. That's what makes and breaks all these things. A potential buyer should look at the race results, whether the car has its original tub, rather than a replacement. It stands to reason that the more original the car is the more valuable it will be. It's a bit like pickaxe heads and handles. There's so little to such cars; there's just the tub and the corners, all of which can be restored and renovated back to as good as new condition. A note should be made of the state of the engine and how many hours it has run.

'Make sure that you have an original chassis plate, because you won't find the number stamped on the tub. In those days you had carnets, which were a nuisance. It would take a couple of weeks, at least, to get a new carnet. Thus it was sometimes easier to swap the identity straight across from one car to another (as happened with the eighth and tenth M23 chassis, M23/8 and M23/8-2).

'The M23 is a car that has competed in the premier league of the sport and been driven by well-known heroes. There is no question that if it is an ex-Hunt or ex-Fittipaldi car, that makes a lot of difference. A World Championship-winning car can be worth around 50% more than one of the others.'

Provenance should be no problem when it comes to McLaren M23s as all 12 survivors have well-documented histories. Although some were, temporarily, converted into show cars by Leo Wybrott, none was initially built as such. All have a full racing history and have been restored to full working condition.

Another possible cause of confusion could be M25/1. As mentioned elsewhere, this was a Formula 5000 car that was virtually converted into an M23. After its working life, it was restored back to F5000 specification with a Chevrolet V8 engine. Now, though, it has been converted back into a DFV-powered 'M23'. This has caused controversy, some purists pointing out that instead of there now being 12 M23s and one unique M25, there are now just 13 M23s, even if the F5000 'restoration' had been far from accurate. However, the value of M25/1 has probably risen simply by virtue of it becoming a Grand Prix car again. One genuine M23 (M23/2) did, temporarily, become a F5000 and then a Can-Am car. However, this has long been back in Formula 1 guise.

Adrian Hamilton was involved in the purchase of one of the most significant of all M23s (M23/8-2), which had been owned by the American, Earl Hartley. 'I can't remember how Dr Hartley and I got together, but I flew over to the States to see him in his house. The car was sitting in the garage with lots of memorabilia. I think that he had bought it directly from the factory. The only reason he was selling this car was because he wanted to buy his daughter a horse. It must have been $75,000 worth of horse. It was not in that bad a nick, so I didn't have to touch it. It was functional, pretty and nicely constructed. I then sold it to Albert Obrist, whose whole collection was eventually swallowed up by Bernie [Ecclestone].'

This is a car to prove his point. 'In the case

of M23/8-2 it is so original and won so many races driven by a young, flamboyant, smoking, drinking, lunatic Englishman.' (It should be pointed out that Hamilton was 'a good mate' of James Hunt.)

Insurance

When it comes to insuring a championship-winning Grand Prix car such as the McLaren M23 there are lots of different factors to take into account, and it's important that the risk is placed with an insurance company that understands the complexities involved with insuring such a unique vehicle.

There are two types of insurance cover available, which allow for (a) the race car to be used on track, and (b) the race car to be covered for storage and transit between circuits, and while garaged by the owner when not being used.

The 'On Track' insurance tends to be an expensive policy, given the risk exposure arising from racing a vehicle on a circuit in a competition. Such cover will usually require the policyholder to accept a high 'excess', this being the amount that the policyholder must pay in the case of a claim against the insurance. The 'excess' would be somewhere in the region of 15–20% of the vehicle value and would allow for most bumps and scrapes endured during competitive motorsport. Underwriters tend to offer lower rates for drivers who agree to accept even higher levels of 'excess'. The cover may often exclude accidents arising from engine failure or from burst tyres, and the detail should always be reviewed before purchase.

The second type of insurance is primarily used to cover the car while it is static. This cover is often referred to as Accidental Damage, Fire and Theft. No cover is provided while the car is under its own power. A feature of the policy offered by Hagerty International, the classic car and bike insurance specialists, is that cover is also provided when the car is in transit between locations such as racetracks and garages that specialise in motorsport preparation. This is because of the high demand for guest appearances of the McLaren M23 at events such as the Silverstone Classic in the UK, Nürburgring Oldtimer Grand Prix in Germany, Spa in Belgium and events that are held further afield, such as at Laguna Seca in the United States of America. If the vehicle is travelling outside the UK or Europe, full details of the journey should be supplied, as a separate policy may be required.

It is of utmost importance that a car of this nature is covered under a specialist policy that offers a previously agreed insurance value should the car be damaged beyond economic repair. This is known as an 'agreed value policy' and it removes any doubt over the value of the vehicle in the event of a claim. In addition, the policy should allow the owner the option to choose his or her own repairer. A specialist vehicle needs specialist care, and companies which provide standard motor insurance could insist that the vehicle is taken to a network of repairers who would not have the knowledge or experience to provide the required service that such a vehicle would warrant. As with all legal contracts (which is essentially what an insurance policy is) the devil is in the detail, so please ensure you always read the small print.

Racing opportunities

All the existing McLaren M23s are based in either Europe or North America, and there are opportunities for owners on both sides of the Atlantic to race them.

The USA could be said to be the birthplace of historic Grand Prix racing. Steve Earle's M23/12 was one of the first to compete there, and a number of other M23s have since taken part in such competitions there. Earle founded the Monterey Historic Automobile Races in

1974, and he ran these annually for 36 years at Laguna Seca, after which they were taken over by the track and renamed the Monterey Motorsports Reunion. This is regarded as the centrepoint of historic racing in North America.

Earle's General Racing has run a number of other events over the years, including the annual Sears Point event, known as the Sonoma Historic Motorsports Festival, which was started 25 seasons ago. He is a strong believer that the 3-litre Grand Prix cars need to be run separately from other cars, 'with their own story board'.

The Historic Grand Prix organisation, which is now headed by James King, was formed as a go-between with the tracks and a body to decide upon regulations with, says Earle, 'safety the absolute'. HGP runs a series of races, not a championship, each year. Earle

describes them as 'lifestyle events'. In 2011 there were six events, but this fell to three in 2012 – the Lime Rock Historic Festival, the US Vintage Grand Prix at Watkins Glen and a support race for the United States Grand Prix at the new Circuit of the Americas in Austin, Texas. As in Europe, there does seem to have been a drop in interest level, with fewer cars as well as fewer races.

The biennial Grand Prix de Monaco Historique is arguably the major European event in which an M23 can still be entered. Prior to 2013, other races in Europe were organised by two separate, UK-based bodies, Historic Formula One (HFO) and Masters Historic Racing. The former, originally known as the Thoroughbred Grand Prix Championship, was sanctioned by the Fédération Internationale de l'Automobile and, in 2012,

BELOW: Three of the USA's four M23s can be seen in this shot from Pocono, including those of Steve Earle, Bill Perrone and Bob Baker's Chesterfield-liveried M23/14.
(Tony Griffiths collection)

was included as a support race for the British Grand Prix. The M23 was eligible for class B, post-1971 non-ground-effect Formula One cars. Having suffered from small grids in its final year, HFO ceased to exist after 2012 and Masters took over as the official FIA championship.

A typical Masters calendar (2013) can include such as the Nürburgring Oldtimer Grand Prix, the Dijon Grand Prix de l'Age d'Or, the Donington Historic Festival and the Silverstone Classic. Classes are named after World Championships of the period, the M23 being eligible for the Fittipaldi (1973–74) and Lauda (1975–77) categories.

On acquiring the car

The time when one might acquire a poor-condition M23, or one that was a non-runner show car, has long gone. However, depending upon what you want to do with the car, there still may be plenty of work to be done. M23/11 had really been Scott Walker's reserve car, not raced recently and lately prepared simply so that it could 'act' in the *Rush!* film. While his M23/6 had been maintained to a high race-prepared state by Hall and Hall, M23/11 needed work if it was to meet the latest historic

race regulations and be an appropriate vehicle for new owner Charles Nearburg to enter for the Grand Prix de Monaco Historique.

Nearburg entrusted the work to Stockbridge-based WDK Motorsport, which had been started just three years previously by directors Kevin Drew, Ian Cox, Simon Turner and Chris Davies. (The fact that WDK stands for 'Wives Don't Know' may reflect something about the high end of historic racing.) At that point it was responsible for seven cars. By the time Nearburg had purchased M23/11 in 2012 it was preparing 30.

Chris Davies listed the work that was scheduled shortly after the acquisition. It was Nearburg's intention to race the car, so there was no question of leaving it in an original state, as might be the case if it were to be only a demonstration or static display car.

All necessary components were crack-tested. In the case of M23/11 it was found that the rear uprights needed replacing. WDK also recommended that new front uprights be fitted, and a new wiring loom. Being out of date, the fuel tanks were replaced, and a new fire extinguisher was installed.

Because M23/11 had been purchased to race, it was crucial to make it suitable for the new driver, which included fitting new seat belts. As it was intended to enter the car for the Monaco Historic Grand Prix and also the FIA-sanctioned Historic Formula One series, there was a need to modify the seat belt mounting to fit a HANS (Head and Neck Support) device. (As yet this is not required in the Masters series.) A mounting was needed inside or on the top of the tub to get the fitting centre right for the device. The cockpit is quite tight and, as Nearburg is not small, there were sharp edges to the fuel tank panel that needed removing, and bolts to be replaced with button heads to make it more comfortable. Shorter bolts were fitted into the cockpit screen for driver comfort. The existing studs were quite long, meaning that they could catch on the driver.

Obviously the battery was replaced, in this case with one from Odyssey. 'We don't tend to have any issues with them,' said Davies. 'There are newer batteries out there, such as the lighter lithium ones, but they are very

BELOW: At this stage M23/11 has only recently arrived at Stockbridge. Hall and Hall had ensured that the car was safe for work on the film set of *Rush!*. Now WDK had to make it race-ready. *(Author)*

expensive and the customers don't necessarily want to pay that.'

Purely for driver comfort, the pedals were moved forward and a new steering column was fitted. The original column had a plug down its centre, which is attached to the kill switch on the steering wheel. 'We will keep that as an original column and then manufacture a new one to the right size for the driver.'

New radius rods were fitted as a matter of course. Equally important were the calipers, which were serviced, including all the pistons being removed and inspected to see that they had not become pitted, and all the seals were replaced. The master and slave cylinders were also serviced and parts were replaced where necessary. The fuel pump mounted on top of the bulkhead was rubbing the roll hoop, so the position needed adjusting to avoid it fretting.

It was known that some of the gauges were already faulty. The temperature and pressure gauges were original Smiths ones, which needed replacing with standard modern versions from Raceparts. The rev counter did not work either, so this was replaced with a chrome one from Stack that looked like the original.

The customer requested a false floor, an extra skin to be fitted to protect the underside of the car. This is simply a sheet of aluminium riveted in place. With no skids on the front, the front bulkhead had collapsed where it had been hitting the floor, and therefore needed repairing. Skid blocks were then put on it to protect it.

When first purchased, there was only one set of magnesium wheels. Those were stripped and crack-checked and will now be used for wet tyres, which do not take as much load. A replica set was then purchased from Barnby Engineering for the slicks.

The M23 has conventional driveshaft joints, not CVs. 'As a matter of course we will replace them,' said Davies. 'We don't know all their history. All the suspension joints, anything that might have any wear in it, was checked and replaced where necessary.'

The airbox was also modified. As previously run, it had gauzes in it, or the trumpets may have had gauzes on top of them. All DFV-engined cars prepared at WDK have an ITG filter on top of them. 'Thus we will modify the airbox so that it fits over the top of the filters. You won't be able to see anything outside.'

As a matter of course, all gear change joints were replaced to take out any slop. Between the back of the tub and the gearbox itself there is no support for gear change. This means that the bar can slightly flex when a gear is changed. About halfway down, WDK added a joint to support the whole system and allow a more positive change.

The radiators were normal copper ones, which were replaced by new aluminium products from Radtec. New oil coolers were fitted, also as a matter of course. The fuel tanks had to come out anyway, so WDK took the opportunity to see how they were arranged and how they worked. 'That meant we would not be in the dark if we got an issue,' remarked Davies.

On arrival, M23/11 did not have a cockpit adjustable brake bias bar, so one of these was fitted. The rain light was not up to current specification, and therefore this was changed. It is not one of those components that can be kept as original if you intend to use the M23 for racing. Likewise a new roll hoop was manufactured to replace the aluminium hoop.

The car has a modern spec Arc starter motor. 'We will bring a mount off the back end of the gearbox just to stop any flexing,' said Davies. 'Checking the starter shaft length is a matter of getting ahead of the game. In the case of M23/11, a bolt needed replacing in the starter shaft.'

The Cosworth DFV had been prepared by Geoff Richardson Racing Engines. The car was also fitted with the later six-speed gearbox. Despite being responsible for the preparation of a number of later DFV-engined Grand Prix cars, this was the first time that WDK had worked on anything other than one with the Hewland five-speed box. The ratios were removed and the layout examined. 'We wanted to find out what was going on inside,' said Davies. The set-up of the gearbox bearing carrier was also checked.

The exhaust pipe at least required repairs to cracks, and areas flattened to clear the bodywork, and the customer was offered the choice of new exhausts.

Thirteen steps to restoring an M23 tub

R& J Simpson Engineering Ltd, of Tamworth, was responsible for restoring the tub of M23/8 for Joaquin Folch-Rusiñol. Director Bob Simpson explains the 13 steps required to carry out the operation.

1 The tub arrived at the factory where it was measured, documented and a jig fitted, locating all of the main pickup points of the car (front bulkhead and engine mounts, etc).

2 Once R & J Simpson was happy that it had gained all the information possible from the existing tub, the process of stripping down the tub into its component panels began. Very little could be salvaged and reused within the new tub.

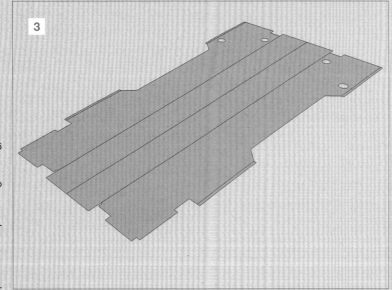

3 The individual panels that needed replacing were then measured and drawn up using CAD, creating a digital copy of all of them. New panels were then laser cut.

4 The new panels were then folded and shaped ready for being fitted into the jig and to each other, using skin pins and clamps.

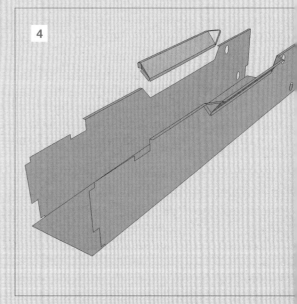

5 A new front bulkhead was fabricated from measurements taken off the existing components, and was bolted on to the jig.

6 Panels fitted to the inner skin.

7 Existing roll-over bar fitted to the new chassis.

8 New dash panel added.

9 Engine mounts and rear panels fitted to the chassis.

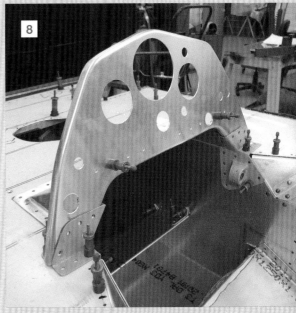

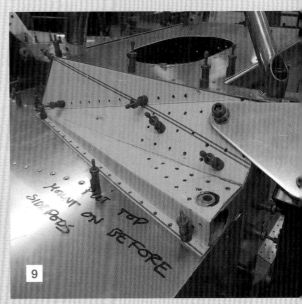

10 More panels added and chassis flipped over for floor fitting.

11 Fibreglass sidepods fitted to the chassis.

12 All panels fitted prior to gluing and riveting together.

13 Completed monocoque.

(all R & J Simpson Engineering)

Historic race preparation

Devon-based Mandarin Motorsport was formed in 2010 by Richard Meins and Chris Livingston-Price, to give them closer control over the costs of maintaining their collections. Meins already owned M23/4 when Mandarin was formed, and since then the car has only been involved in running and general maintenance. The experienced Adam Brock, who runs the operation, has been working on historic cars for about eight years, finding that this is where his real passion is. He explained the work carried out when preparing an M23 for a historic race.

'Typically, we will take the bearing carrier off the back of the gearbox, take the ratios out and inspect them, also the dog rings and the forks. We will strip all four corners, and clean the calipers. Depending upon the race and the point in the season we will probably take the gearbox off the car and check, and possibly replace, the clutch. We clean up the face of the flywheel. We take the rear driveshafts off, strip them, clean and regrease, and do the same with the wheel bearings. Every third race, we strip and reseal the brake calipers. Everything should be spanner checked. When everything is put back together, fresh brake and clutch fluid should be pumped through. You should change the engine oil, and fill with fresh coolant, and fresh oil in the gearbox when you make your ratio selection for the next race. Drain the fuel out and then put an appropriate amount of fuel back in. We normally keep about five litres of fuel in to keep the tank wet when the car is not being used.

'We have a rule that the car does not go into the truck until it is race-ready. We put the right tyres on with the correct pressures, and ensure that we have the right quantity of fuel. We have a pre-heater on the McLaren that pre-heats the water. That is put on for an hour before the car is due to go out, pre-heating to about 70–80°. The heat soak into the oil then gets that up to about 30–40°. The car is then fired up on full rich using the mixture adjuster on the metering unit. Then we warm it so that it revs crisp and clean. At most circuits it is usually one off full lean. At places like Spa and Dijon we run full lean because of the atmosphere.

'In free practice the driver will usually do five laps and in. The tyre pressures should then be checked to see if they are coming up to temperature. There may be some subtle wing or damper changes depending on how the driver feels. After qualifying, a full spanner check will take place, pretty much every single nut and bolt on the car. We wash the brake calipers out with brake cleaner, bleed the brakes and the clutch and pump in fresh fluid and check all levels. We also drain the fuel out, thus enabling us to work out how much has been used. Knowing how long the race will be, we can then put the appropriate amount back in, plus a little bit extra – "the mechanic's gallon".

'Prior to starting we squirt a little bit of petrol down each trumpet, just to wet it. Then it is a matter of turning the electric fuel pump on, turning the ignition on and pressing the starter. Once it fires, the mechanical injection starts injecting fuel. There is an adjuster on the metering unit with five settings. Put this on full rich to start with. Once you rev it, it will either rev clean or it won't, so you keep it on that setting until it does. Then you can go to the next setting until you have your race setting.'

BELOW: Adam Brock at work on M23/4.
(Author)

The Cosworth DFV in historic racing

There is a particular link between the 3-litre Cosworth DFVs used by the McLaren factory team in the 1970s and the availability of such engines for historic racing: Nicholson McLaren, the company formed by McLaren to develop its own DFVs. The now Wokingham-based company still services DFVs, as well as restoring old ones. Richard Meins's M23/4 is one McLaren that continues to race with a Nicholson McLaren DFV, while M23/5, which resides in the foyer at McLaren International, also has such an engine.

After its Grand Prix life was over, the DFV became the initial power unit for Formula 3000 when the category was introduced in 1985. The DFV powered the European F3000 champions for four seasons before being eclipsed by a Mugen Honda engine. 'When the Cosworth DFV was no longer the engine of choice for Formula 3000, we were left with a lot of short-stroke versions,' recalled John Nicholson. 'I don't think that the Historic Formula One series had sufficient long-stroke engines to keep its series going, so the short-strokes were slowly introduced into it. [Fellow engine tuner] Heini Mader and I must have introduced about 40. The short-stroke is more powerful, but there are some people who prefer to retain the [historically correct] long-stroke engine to keep the car genuine.

'The strongest engines in HFO are probably our short-strokers, but they have got our own components such as cams and valves. Power

output is now at least 520hp at 10,500 revs whereas, before, the engines used to rev to 11,000.'

'Many of the engines we see now can have been lying around for a long time, and then we have to offer a restoration service,' says Nicholson McLaren sales director John Waghorn. 'That involves salvaging blocks and heads. With modern welding techniques there is a lot more now that can be saved. We have to identify what customers want in terms of pump layout, will it fit their chassis – which can be a bit of an issue, whether they want long- or short-stroke and so on. We refresh engines for McLaren International, where we deal with Neil Trundle, if it wants to run a car from its collection.'

Servicing the Cosworth DFV

The engine can be the most expensive aspect of historic Formula 1 racing, so it is crucial to use the services of a Cosworth DFV specialist, of which a number, such as Langford Performance Engineering and Geoff Richardson Racing, as well as Nicholson McLaren, still exist.

On arrival at Nicholson McLaren's base, a Cosworth DFV will be stripped down completely. It will then go through a cleaning process and be visually inspected and crack-tested, using either DPI (dye penetrant inspection) or magnaflux (magnetic particle inspection). Con rods are checked for bends and twists. Pistons are tending to last for two rebuilds but are crack-

BELOW: Fresh brake and clutch fluid should be pumped through. (Author)

BELOW MIDDLE: Everything should be spanner checked. (Author)

BELOW RIGHT: The adjuster on the metering unit has five settings. (Author)

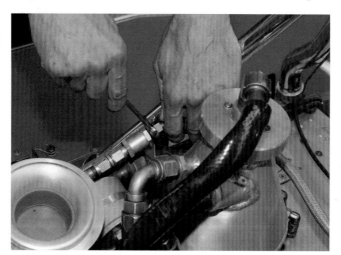

ABOVE: 2012 meets 1976 – Scott Walker (left) with Alastair Caldwell. *(Nichola Aigner)*

tested and inspected and replaced, if necessary, each time. 'More and more, we are finding evidence of cracks on blocks, but we now usually have the technology to repair them. In period you would probably have just put a new block in,' says Nicholson.

Measuring the main bearing tunnels is then one of the first operations to take place. The number two and number four journals tend to fret; the bearings fitted were very heavy. The main bearing clearance on the crank can increase, leading to a higher oil flow. That means more drag, less power. A line bore could be necessary to overcome this. The liner registers distort in the same way as the main tunnels. In which case, these would have to be bored again and an oversize liner fitted.

'We have the facilities to replace valve guides and valve seats, and also to repair cylinder heads, if required,' says Nicholson. 'The cam carriers can be a weak point, so we have techniques for servicing them. Good useable replacements are very hard to come by. Metering units are serviced in house, as are spark boxes, for which we have test rigs.' These are the first of the major sub-assemblies to be removed from the engine.

A total rebuild can take around 120 hours.

If the engine is in first-class condition, the pistons and valve springs will be the only major components that need replacing, along with various consumables and service items. The pistons are matched to the bores, machined twice to set squish height and then to determine the compression ratio. Each piston will have to weigh within a gram of the other seven. The con rods, each of which will be tested to ensure there is no imbalance between the big and small ends, will also have to match in like fashion.

Should a DFV have been over-revved, then the big-end bolts will require replacing. This problem will show up on the pistons, valves, and valve springs, and as traces of white metal clinging to the scavenge filters.

Another item requiring work will be the two oil pumps. Rotors and seals will be replaced, the castings crack-tested and the various small parts reassembled. The rotors will be cleaned up and matched to their housings.

The engine will then be reassembled, dyno tested and finally examined for any signs of dyno damage, such as a broken valve spring or indications that a piston or bearing has picked up. Should this have occurred, the engine will, naturally, be taken down again and the problem rectified.

ABOVE: Nicholson McLaren was the in-house supplier to the M23 and still provides engines for such cars racing today. *(Author)*

The owner's view

Scott Walker (M23/6 and M23/11)

'I already had a McLaren M19, the very best one, so I was a fan of McLaren,' said European businessman Scott Walker, whose M23 is prepared by Hall and Hall. 'I acquired it about ten years ago and raced it for a couple of years. However, 1976 was the year that I saw my first race live. That was when Lauda came back at Monza. During that period I was a fan of Niki Lauda because I was born in a village close to the Ferrari factory. At Monza I saw not only the Ferrari of Lauda but also the McLaren M23 of James Hunt, who was trying to catch him up to win the World Championship.

'Apart from the Ferrari, I considered the M23 the best car of the mid-1970s. I had been looking around for an M23 for a long period because it was not easy to find one. I wanted to run a Cosworth car because of the difficulty of finding spares for a Ferrari. Then I got the possibility to acquire a big history M23, chassis number six. I acquired it from a British lady [Lorina McLaughlin] who had had the car for a long time. We met at Monaco and we kept in touch because she was not very keen on selling

ABOVE: Rob Hall sits in one of Scott Walker's M23s, to which camera equipment has been installed for the filming of *Rush!*. (Jon Bunston)

THE HALL WAY

Bourne-based Hall and Hall had already been looking after M23/6 when Scott Walker purchased it from David and Lorina McLaughlin. Rob Hall recalled that Scott Walker took in a few races in 2007. 'At the end of the season the old girl was a bit tired.' Thus the car was completely stripped down. The tub was taken to pieces and a new floor, new seat and fuel tank, plus two inner panels fitted. New suspension was also installed. Scott Walker, though, kept all the old parts.

'It ended up being a bigger job than we thought,' said Hall. 'The crash structures had to be taken off. Kerry Adams had the moulds that enabled new ones to be made.' The time before its next race at Mugello ended up as being so short that the monocoque appeared there in virginal white with the correct logos but no red livery. Next up was Monaco, by which time M23/6 looked as it should. The car has been raced less in recent times, although it did appear at the joint race/*Rush!* film shoot at the Nürburgring late in 2011. Hall and Hall then made the car ready for the main shooting in 2012. It may not have been James Hunt's car in real life, but it would be for the movie.

Scott Walker then brought M23/11, which was the same configuration as his other car but, as Hall remembered, 'had not been looked at for years'. It needed recommissioning if it was to be safe enough for the film, and crack-testing was carried out. All the bag tanks were removed, leaving just the seat tank. The car's existing Cosworth DFV refused to start, so Hall and Hall took one from its own stock. The gearbox was also rebuilt. M23/6 had an earlier five-speed box; not so M23/11. 'It was the first six-speed for a DFV that I had seen,' said Hall. Shortly after filming had finished Hall and Hall sold M23/11 for Scott Walker to Charles Nearburg. Hall recalled how the deal was done over the weekend of the Goodwood Revival meeting.

'The M23s are just great cars. You could not get a stronger, more robust one,' he said.

the car. It was not a matter of price, but she had owned the car a long time. There was a big parade on the Champs-Elysées in Paris for an FIA anniversary and I saw the car again there. I was in love with it and we did the deal in 2006.

'I started to race it in the Historic Formula One series. At first I had to understand the car; the handling was different from the M19. The M23 was very physical, but I loved it because you could really feel the car. It was fantastic. I was able to gain confidence and trust in the car. It's a very predictable car. When you brake, it stops and you don't see any locking of the wheels. When you are on fast tracks like Monza, the feeling is very, very good.

'Most of my experience before was with sports cars of the 1950s. I raced an ex-Mike Hawthorn Ferrari 750 Monza for many years. My favourite cars are the front-engined, drum-braked sports cars of the 1950s or the Formula 1cars of the 1970s.

'I was very happy in 2008 when I finished fifth at Monaco, even though I was hit in the back by another car at Mirabeau. There were some very fast drivers in front.

'I acquired the second car (chassis number 11) from the United States in 2008. In 2005 I had had the opportunity to buy either a M19 or M23/11 at the same price, but because I only wanted the best history car, I decided to buy the M19. But then I fell in love with driving the M23; I decided it would be a good investment to have two M23s. In case something wrong happened to one chassis, the other one would be available. Last but not least, because chassis number six has a big history maybe I would use the other chassis more. I have only raced '6', though, but the other has been got ready, and the first time out since I owned it was in the *Rush!* film, where it was driven by Jochen Mass.' (Scott Walker was subsequently to sell M23/11 to Charles Nearburg.)

'I was on holiday in California with the family when I had a call about the film at three in the morning. It was explained to me quickly what it was about, and I was super happy because I had been living these years and owned two of the cars from these years. It was amazing, I have been playing James Hunt… with the helmet on, of course.'

Steve Earle M23/12

It has been said that Steve Earle, the founder of the annual Monterey Historic Automobile Races (or Monterey Motorsports Reunion as it is now known), legitimised the historic Formula 1 movement when he purchased McLaren M23/12. A number of 3-litre Grand Prix cars had found their way to the USA by the late 1970s but, initially, there was little enthusiasm to do anything with them. In the mid-1980s they could be picked up for as little as $40,000 to $50,000. The historic Formula 1 movement grew in America and then in Europe, with a number of the cars making their way back there. At one point, seven M23s were based in the USA (M23/3, M23/8, M23/8-2, M23/9, M23/11, M23/12 and M23/14), although M23/8, M23/8-2 and M23/11 returned to Europe.

'Harley Cluxton told me that he had bought one from McLaren in 1978 and that he was thinking of building it into a Can-Am car. It had been Mass's car in 1977 and had made its debut at Long Beach. It had only done six races, and I think was the one car that Mass hadn't crashed that year! When I bought it in 1986 it was pretty virginal. It was a true transition car, as bits and pieces of it were M26. Initially, I had an early DFV, number 940, which had run in a Tyrrell.'

Corte Madera-based Phil Reilly, North America's leading historic Formula 1 specialist,

ABOVE: Steve Earle at Sonoma, the historic racing festival organised by his company. *(Steve Earle collection)*

who was to run the car, checked it over. Former Grand Prix driver Pete Lovely, who was also in at the start of historic F1 racing, and Gary Gove who worked with him, also took an interest. Gove took it out on the track and reported, 'This car, right now, is really good.'

'If it was a good car to begin with, I was going to live with that,' recalled Earle. It was also important to him 'to maintain its historical integrity'. A second, later engine was eventually purchased, and the original DFV sold.

Despite having entered and raced sports cars – he was to compete at such as Le Mans, Daytona and Sebring – the M23 was Earle's first experience of an open-wheel car. Running it at Sears Point, 'I learnt to get confident in it. I loved it, although I was to learn that it had a heavy feel. I became conscious that the other guys who had experienced M23s said they were more physical to drive. I also didn't realise how rough the DFV was until I tried an ex-Niki Lauda Ferrari 312 T2. Compared to the Ferrari, the McLaren seemed to have each of its corners put together by a different guy. However, at this level of competition such things don't make any difference.'

On one occasion, Indianapolis 500-winner Bobby Rahal drove the M23 for Earle at Elkhart Lake. Rahal had driven the final two Grands Prix of 1978 in a Wolf. According to Earle, Rahal

had been offered the opportunity of a race in an M23 that year. He had been told that the M23 was a good car but had not quite realised just how much better it was than the Wolf until he had driven Earle's example many years later.

'It was a great car in which you could control your own destiny. In historic racing you should drive at the level you are most comfortable at, and run with the guys you want.

'I was successful in the M23 for about ten years, but then the competition became too intense. I gradually made my way from the front to the middle of the pack. About four years ago I had one of those maturing moments and sold the car to Richard Griot. He seemed really excited about it, but then he only ran it twice and it has been in the garage ever since. He's got a wonderful car.'

Joaquin Folch-Rusiñol M23/8

Spanish businessman and former motorcycle racer Joaquin Folch-Rusiñol turned to car racing with an Aston Martin DB4 and then a Lotus 23. 'I was told that I must go to single-seaters because they were much more enjoyable than anything else. I was lent a Lotus 27 Formula Junior for one race, and that winter I bought one myself, competing the Lurani Trophy for two years. In 1996 I was lent a Williams FW08 for a race at Dijon. I nearly bought that car, but I was advised by some of the members of Thoroughbred Grand Prix, as it was then, not to as, having never been raced in period, it would not be eligible the following year. Then Sean Walker told me he was selling his Lotus 87B, so I bought that instead. I raced that until 2002.'

From there, other Grand Prix cars followed. '2002 to 2006 were very good years. In 2005, Bernie [Ecclestone] asked why I wasn't driving a Brabham. He then told me to borrow one (a BT49C) from his collection!

'The reason I bought the McLaren M23, as well as an M19, Ferrari T3 and a Lotus 16 was because they were eligible to compete at Monaco. An M23 was the last winning car at Montjuich Park in Barcelona, even if it was a half Grand Prix. I acquired the car through David Clark at a very reasonable price. I phoned Simon Hadfield, who runs some of my cars, and he advised me, "Just buy it. It was a car ahead of its time. It's also an ex-Emerson

Fittipaldi car with lots of history. You can do a lot of things with it: Masters, HFO in class D, and you can do Monaco."

'Also, for me, a good-looking car is a plus when it comes to choosing it.

'The M23 has a fantastic package. In 2005 at the Nürburgring with Masters – I race with Masters and HFO; any series that will welcome me – we had a bad beginning to the weekend, making contact with a Wolf. One of the radiators was damaged. Simon said we would not be able to race. The night before the race it rained heavily, and on the Sunday morning the track was wet, wet, wet. By that I mean wet by Nürburgring standards, in other words, overflowing. Simon called me at the hotel and asked if I wanted to race because in those conditions it was possible to do so with just one radiator. I said, "Why not? We're here." It meant I had to start from the bottom of the grid, and we won the race. The car in the wet was something incredible. It was very soft, had lots of torque. At Monaco in 2008 we had a magnificent race with Duncan Dayton in his Brabham BT33; we were so close.

'If you enjoy motor racing you have a good memory of each car, and probably the best memory is the last one.'

Folch-Rusiñol bought the M23 when he was racing a Williams FW08, and at the time these and the older cars were prepared and run by Simon Hadfield Motorsports. Since then Folch-Rusiñol has spilt his operation so that Hadfield continues to run his Lotus 16 and Maserati 250F, while the newer cars have, since 2006, been run by Fredy Kumschick's company in Switzerland, Kumschick Racing. 'I think that, as an amateur driver, if you can have two providers, that's good.

'When I bought it, Simon asked what configuration I wanted it to be in. I answered, as it was when it won the Spanish Grand Prix... because I was there!' said Folch-Rusiñol. 'We changed some panels where the riveting was loose, but basically the tub is still original. We replaced the side panels, especially the ones that were supporting the uprights, and we could feel the difference. The car was so much stronger; it was reactive to any change we did with the settings. This is when you feel that the tub is strong.'

John Anderson M23/3

John Anderson's love affair with the McLaren M23 began almost immediately following its 'sensational debut' in South Africa. 'Dennis Hulme was already a big hero. So was Jody Scheckter, who came to the USA to drive in F5000. I'd never seen a big car driven that hard before.'

In the late 1980s, Anderson found himself looking after a car collection at Sears Point raceway and maintaining McLaren M23/14. 'In 1991, I went to New Zealand and visited Dennis. I remember seeing his M23, which was parked precariously in his garage under an overladen shelf of camping gear!'

About three years later, Bruce Treney, who runs the Fantasy Junction in Emeryville, California, asked Anderson to carry out an appraisal of M23/3, which was then at the Matsuda Collection in Japan. At the time it was thought to be a different M23, but 'we took the right side of the car and found the repairs that Leo [Wybrott] indicated had been carried out after Jody's [Silverstone] accident. We started to strip the paint off and found underneath the original Yardley colours. The car also had the original chassis tag.'

Anderson decided to buy the car himself, selling the Alfa Romeo Giulietta with which he had won an SCCA National Championship in 1977, plus a Formula Ford, to do so. 'That just gave me enough to buy the McLaren. At that time my job was just about disappearing, so I had to go home and tell my wife that I had not only just lost my job but also bought this car.'

Thankfully, his wife Carol Spears is an enthusiast and 'thought it a better idea than I did!'

Anderson restored the car in his workshop at Sears Point. 'The M23 had been a Marlboro show car and was painted with James Hunt's name on the side and Andrea de Adamich's on the front wing (de Adamich drove the Alfa-Romeo-engined M7D and M14Ds for McLaren in 1970.) It also featured crude sidepod extensions and a low airbox. It came with a hollow DFV and a hollow gearbox. It had remained pretty much unmolested. It had been on and off trailers and we ended up rebuilding about a third of the floor. We rebuilt the rear wing.

'Both Leo Wybrott, who told me that he had rebuilt the car after Jody's accident, and Kerry Adams, who provided the proper airbox and paint colours, were very helpful. Phil Kerr, who I had got to know through Dennis, was also very encouraging. Paul Reilly, who is responsible for the majority of DFVs in the USA, built up an early specification Cosworth.' The core engine was believed to have come from the Interscope Penske raced by Danny Ongais in 1977. The Hewland gearbox main case was 'in excellent condition', enabling Anderson to build the 'box up himself. Australian Ian Gordon, a former Brabham mechanic, assisted with the fabrication.

'I'm just a mechanic, so it took me a while to get it done, but I finished rebuilding the car in 2002/2003 and took it to the Monterey Historic meeting at Laguna Seca.' Other tracks followed, including Montreal and Watkins Glen. The latter was 'a memorable experience. I'd always wanted to go through the esses there in a Grand Prix car.'

After five years, Anderson sold M23/3 to Bob Baker of Sun Valley, Idaho, who already had M23/14. 'You have to be a man of means to keep such a car,' observed Anderson, although he does still own Tyrrell 007. 'I also drive a Wolf for one of my customers. All three of them Jody raced and wrecked!' There seems to be a theme here.

Richard Meins M23/4

Richard Meins combines modern GT racing with historics. He entered the latter scene in about 2002, because he was 'a little bit fed up of spending a lot of money on modern racing'

and he purchased a Ford GT40. Prior to this point he had never raced a single-seater. Ron Maydon, the founder and president of the Master series, suggested that he try a Surtees TS19 run by Hall and Hall, which resulted in winning one of his first races with it at Spa. 'I just loved it. It changed my attitude to Formula 1 cars. I had assumed that they were difficult to drive.'

'I had always loved the McLaren. That M23 has got to be one of the most attractive looking cars, not to mention one of the most successful. I kept my eyes open, and then this car, which was owned by Abba Kogan, came up for sale. He hadn't raced it for a year or so but the car was fine.

'I started racing it with Simon Blake of Historic Automobiles, a fantastic preparer. However, it made sense to Chris Livingston-Price and I to have our own workshop for our collections and try to get some cost control. So, we decided to start Mandarin Motorsport and brought Adam Brock on board.

'I began to race it regularly. It wasn't the most competitive car because people were running such as 1977–79 Marches and Wolfs, and we had a long-stroke engine, but we could hang on the back of the first four or five. That was in the dry; when it rained, we won! It's a lovely car, for its time it's amazing. It's like driving a kart. The Williams feels like it is on rails where the McLaren isn't. It will move around a bit. I had an enjoyable couple of years with it and we also had Emerson Fittipaldi drive it in the 2010 Goodwood Festival of Speed. It was the first time that he had sat in an M23 since 1975. Martin Brundle also drove it for the BBC before a Grand Prix broadcast. You can still see that on YouTube.

'Then Ron Maydon decided to open Masters up to ground-effect cars. We fell back to mid-pack. I didn't enjoy it as much. You might not win, but at least you want to be at the right end of it. So, I bought a Williams FW07 and, for a while, stopped racing the M23. Cars I have, I tend to use, so I think I will still enter the odd race in the future. It's such a beautiful car, and I am hoping to home it in my new garage/office. Some people like paintings, I prefer an M23.'

BELOW: Richard Meins at the 2008 Silverstone Classic.
(Author)

Greg Galdi M23/9

'I purchased M23/9 from Leo Wybrott. So, in effect, I'm the first owner since the factory,' said New York-based entrepreneur Greg Galdi. 'It had been in the Brooklands Museum for 25 years, and on a visit there a few years ago they were dismayed that it had left to go to 'some stateside chap'. At that time I had considered a Lotus 72. However, my friend Neil Trundle helped me decide otherwise. The timing was right, as Leo was retiring and moving to Australia, and offered up his M23. I acquired it around the turn of the millennium. It was wonderfully original with hand-painted decals and a steering wheel engraved with 'Hunt – M23/8-2'. Kerry Adams did a terrific restoration, and Nicholson McLaren refreshed their engine already installed, but I haven't touched the bodywork. The metal tub had been expanded a bit, fortunately for me.

'I have raced it at such as Laguna Seca (the Monterey historic meeting), Road America and Mount Tremblant, as well as, almost every year, Watkins Glen. I have childhood memories of seeing these cars there. Nearly always this is with Historic Grand Prix where there is a discipline and a sense of understanding that "the cars are the stars".' In 2012 Galdi ran the car in a supporting race for the US Grand Prix at the new Austin track in Texas, an event for which he had the highest praise.

'The car is very happy when it is stretching its legs. I'm in the mid-pack, but I'm driving a piece

of history. Even so, I experience 2.0 to 2.5g.'

Galdi owns a number of racing cars, including an ex-Derek Bell Porsche 956, original unraced Porsche 917 and an ex-Didier Pironi Tyrrell 009 from 1979. He compares the two Grand Prix cars, pointing out that the M23 has more of a feeling of 'keeling over'. 'You get a feel of that lean. The Tyrrell corners and brakes in a flatter attitude.'

'I'm on the board of the museum at the International Motor Racing Research Center in Watkins Glen. I offered it to them for a few weeks in 2012 and it stayed there for four months.' The display was a cap to the Center's year-long celebration of the 50th anniversary of the first Formula 1 race at Watkins Glen.

TOP: Not James Hunt, not even Scott Walker on the set for *Rush!*, but Greg Galdi in the supporting race for the inaugural Grand Prix at Austin, Texas. *(Mark Coughlin)*

ABOVE: Greg Galdi's M23/9 on display at Watkins Glen during 2012. *(Nicholas Phoenix)*

A STARRING ROLE

McLaren M23s again became stars with the making of the feature film, *Rush!*, which was scheduled for launch in 2013. The film chronicles the battle for the 1976 World Championship between James Hunt and Niki Lauda, with racing scenes shot during 2012 at a variety of locations from Blackbushe Airport to the Nürburgring and Donington Park.

Three genuine M23s appear, as do two replicas. Stuart McCrudden, who had formerly run the Historic Formula One series became the historic vehicle co-ordinator, initially identifying the cars of the period and then sourcing the current owners, as well as assisting in the training of the actors and organising the cars on the sets. The film's co-producer Jim Hajicosta recalled how he had first approached McCrudden and HFO chairman Dan Collins. 'I told them that we were making a film about motor racing, and they thought I was full of hot air. At that point there was a different director on board. Two weeks later I had to tell them that we had lost the director. About a month later, though, we had we new one, [two times Academy award winner] Ron Howard.'

The film required at least two M23s. Scott Walker had a pair, but McCrudden recalled that one of them was 'a basket case'.

'When we first met Scott Walker I hadn't realised he had two of them,' said Hajicosta. The producers agreed to underwrite the preparation of the latter at Hall and Hall. Scott Walker was thus able to portray James Hunt in the racing scenes, while, appropriately, the Jochen Mass car was driven in some of the scenes by Mass himself. A third M23 appears in a 1973 paddock shot. Kerry Adams brought along Jody Scheckter's car to ensure that this was in the correct Yardley colour scheme. This attention to detail was also reflected in the manufacture of two high airboxes for Scott Walker's car so that they would appear correct in the early races of 1976. 'Originally, the visual effects company did not want us to make them, but we overruled them,' recalled Hajicosta. At one stage the producers spoke to Richard Meins about using M23/4, as it would be correct for a 1975 race scene; an idea eventually shelved.

Adams was not the only contemporary McLaren mechanic to visit the set of the film. Alastair Caldwell, David Luff and Roy Reader also attended, and they were employed to advise the pit crew extras.

The two McLaren M23s were built by WDK Motorsport, which coincidentally, after the film was finished, was to take over the running of M23/11 following its sale to Charles Nearburg. Max Byrne headed the project, with WDK building three replicas for the film, although, by altering its bodywork, one of the 'McLarens' could be changed into a 'Brabham' or a 'Hesketh'.

Both M23 replicas were based on old Formula Vauxhall Lotus cars with extended wheelbases. The look of the car was achieved by aluminium panel work, along with fibreglass airboxes and noses. 'We made fibreglass moulds of the DFV cam covers and the backs of the engines,' said WDK's Chris Davies. 'We have so many real DFVs here! We also made dummy

BELOW: Stuart McCrudden not only sourced the cars for *Rush!* but also masterminded their on-set activity.
(Nichola Aigner)

BOTTOM: Spot the real thing. Max Byrne works on a Formula Vauxhall-based replica, with the genuine article in the background.
(Nichola Aigner)

injectors within dummy trumpets, injector lines, dummy spark box, distributor cap and leads, dummy exhausts on one side, the other being the real exhaust exit for the Vauxhall engine. Two painted wooden MDF brake discs were made for the rear, and dummy calipers manufactured from aluminium. The fact that detail shots would be taken meant that the dashboards had to look accurate. We also had to find a way of mounting a dummy radius rod to the upright that would still move up and down.

'It was an interesting project,' said Davies. 'The timescales kept changing, so it was quite a lot of hard work and a few late nights.'

ABOVE: Ron Howard, director of such films as *Apollo 13*, *Cocoon* and *A Beautiful Mind*, would refer to the McLarens as the 'red and white cars'.
(Nichola Aigner)

LEFT: The M23s grew cameras for *Rush!*.
(Jon Bunston)

LEFT: Scott Walker's pair of M23s on set at Blackbushe Airport.
(Nichola Aigner)

'I know what I want out of my car.'

James Hunt
Marlboro Team Texaco driver 1976 to 1978

(LAT)

Chapter Six

Individual chassis histories

Thirteen genuine M23s were built, of which 12 can still be seen today. Two were raced as privateer cars, with one of them being specifically built as such. Subsequent lives have been varied; some became show cars, one even spent a while as a V8-engined Formula 5000 and then as a Can-Am car. However, all apart from Hailwood's Nürburgring-accident car are now back to original specification.

A total of 13 McLaren M23s were built. A 14th car, the F5000 M25 was, to all intents, temporarily converted into an M23. Alastair Caldwell reminds us that teams would swap chassis numbers for convenience when transporting them across borders, and that during his time McLaren was no exception, leading to inaccuracies appearing in the contemporary press. However, Kerry Adams reckoned that McLaren was one of the least offenders.

Confusion can arise over the fact that two cars have been known as M23/8. The eighth chassis built (M23/8) became, for a time, M23/10, while the tenth chassis to be manufactured (M23/8-2) was never known as M23/10, but either M23/8-2 or even at one point M23/8!

M25/1 was sometimes confusingly referred to as M25/23-1 by the press. It was even mistakenly called M23/7. What happened to the parts of the real M23/7 is a controversial story, but what can be told is that the tub ended its days as a training tool for the Brands Hatch marshals. All the other M23s still officially exist.

A number of the cars were converted into show cars for Marlboro and Texaco. This has led to historic race organisers refusing entry on the misunderstanding that they had never raced. All the show cars had, however, started their lives as genuine race cars.

M23/1

The first of the M23s, M23/1 was built in 1973. With Denny Hulme driving, it achieved pole position and led its first ever race, the 1973 South African Grand Prix. Hulme drove it throughout 1973, winning the Swedish Grand Prix with it. It remained Yardley liveried for the start of 1974 when Mike Hailwood drove it. It became the Yardley spare following the build of M23/7, but was crashed by Hailwood in practice for the German Grand Prix.

Denny Hulme eventually took the car to New Zealand, where he occasionally made high-speed demonstrations. 'When Denny left the company to go back to New Zealand, we totally rebuilt M23/1, with Denny helping. It had a lot of good new stuff built into it,' recalled Leo Wybrott. After Hulme's death, it became the Bruce McLaren Trust car and was put on display in Te Puke. In 2006, Hulme's widow Greeta sold it to Christchurch-based Phil Mauger. John Crawford stripped and restored the car for Mauger, using many of the original parts. Coincidentally, Mauger's namesake Ivan Mauger, the former multiple World Speedway Champion, recalled being shown over the car by Hulme in 1972.

M23/2

M23/2 made its debut at the 1973 Silverstone International Trophy with Peter Revson at the wheel. The American then used it for much of the season, winning the British Grand Prix with it at the same track. It was taken over by Jody Scheckter for the last two Grands Prix of the year.

The car then went to South Africa, where it was raced privately by Dave Charlton. The Yorkshire-born Charlton added to the

BELOW: M23/1 was very much Denny Hulme's car, and it went with him when he returned to New Zealand. This is Monza in 1973. *(Ford)*

four consecutive South African Drivers' Championship titles that he had won with a pair of Lotuses by taking the title again in 1974 and 1975 using the M23. Charlton also used it in the South African Grand Prix during those years.

It remained outside of Europe, going next to Australia where former New Zealand Grand Prix winner John McCormack ran it as a Leyland V8-powered F5000 car. As such, it was the only genuine M23 to race with anything other than a DFV engine. McCormack campaigned it from 1977 to 1978, winning the Australian Drivers' Championship in 1977. He also fitted enveloping bodywork to compete in three Can-Am races in the USA in 1979.

It was then purchased, via Leo Wybrott, for McLaren's own collection and rebuilt in Yardley colours. Meanwhile, former McLaren mechanic Kerry Adams was trying to buy, for Jody Scheckter, M23/3 (which the South African had crashed at Silverstone) from John Anderson. 'I tried for many years to get it from John and he was having none of it. However, he did say we could have first refusal if it ever did go for sale, because he knew who I wanted to buy it for,' said Adams.

Adams had also tried to buy an ex-Scheckter M19 from Mary Foulston, but again with no luck. Instead he purchased another M19 from Howden Ganley for Jody. Then the Foulston car did come up for sale, so Scheckter instructed Adams to buy that as well.

At this time, Adams was restoring M23/5 for McLaren. He contacted Ron Dennis to point out that Scheckter had the two M19s, while McLaren did not have one in its collection. M23/2 was also in Yardley colours, which did not sit well with a Marlboro theme. A like-for-like swap was suggested. The DFV was taken out of M23/2, put into the outgoing M19, and another purchased for the car. The car is now kept on Scheckter's estate in a private museum. The only time it has turned a wheel since was when it appeared at the 2012 CarFest, which was held at the Scheckters' Laverstoke Park Farm, driven by Jody's son, former IndyCar driver Thomas Scheckter.

M23/3

Built in 1973, M23/3 was used by Jody Scheckter to make his European Formula 1 debut in France. It was also driven by the South African at that year's British Grand Prix (the first where three M23s were on the grid), where he started the infamous Woodcote crash.

The car was repaired after that incident and became a Marlboro show car before being acquired by the Matsuda Collection in Japan. It was later bought by John Anderson and restored at his workshop in Sears Point, California. After five years, Anderson sold it on to the enthusiastic octogenarian Bob Baker from Idaho, who still enters it for racing.

M23/4

M23/4 was originally the McLaren team's spare for the 1973 Dutch Grand Prix, and was first raced by guest Jacky Ickx in Germany. Revson used it to win that year's Canadian Grand Prix. It was also the team spare at the start of the next year, driven by both Hulme and Fittipaldi,

but was eventually resprayed in Yardley livery, following the loss of M23/1 and M23/7 in Germany, for David Hobbs and Jochen Mass to drive. Back in Marlboro colours, it had just three outings in 1975, with Mass crashing it at Silverstone and on the first lap at the Nürburgring.

It was effectively written off but rebuilt as a non-running promotional show car for Marlboro. Former Grand Prix driver Andrea de Adamich, who had done a deal to market a range of Marlboro-branded sportswear, then acquired it, and it was returned to England to be rebuilt to full running condition by Woking-based Grand Prix Engineering, a new venture established by Dermot Walsh and Ron Dennis to work on historic McLarens. As a show car, M23/4 had been in 1975 livery, but was returned to 1974 Marlboro colours as part of the restoration.

Andrea de Adamich was to sell it to Monaco-based Brazilian collector Abba Kogan in 1999. He entered it for Thoroughbred Grand Prix and GP Masters events over a number of years before selling it in 2006 to shipping broker Richard Meins, who has continued to race it, winning on a number of occasions. It was driven by Emerson Fittipaldi at the 2010 Goodwood Festival of Speed.

M23/5

M23/5 was built during the winter of 1973/74, its first Grand Prix being at Buenos Aires, where Emerson Fittipaldi raced it. The Brazilian used it in the first half of that season, winning the

Brazilian and Belgian Grands Prix. The car, which has been restored by Kerry Adams, is still owned by McLaren and is now on display at the McLaren Technology Centre in Woking.

M23/6

M23/6 was also built during the winter of 1973/74 and driven during the year by Denny Hulme, the New Zealander using it to win the Argentine Grand Prix. It became Fittipaldi's spare car for 1975, replacing M23/9 in South Africa when the latter blew its engine in practice. Likewise, it was driven by Mass in Zolder after he had crashed M23/8. It became Mass's usual car towards the end of the season, and in 1976 was driven both by Mass and sometimes by Hunt, who used it to win in France and Germany.

The following season it was campaigned by private entrant Emilio de Villota, running it in the British national Formula 1 series as well as attempting to qualify for Grands Prix.

M23/6 subsequently came into the hands of the husband and wife team of David and Lorina McLaughlin, and was raced by Lorina. A highlight of this period was when she drove the car on a nine-kilometre route around the centre of Paris as part of the celebrations of 100 years of French Grand Prix racing. It is now owned by businessman Scott Walker and prepared by Hall and Hall in Bourne.

M23/7

Chassis M23/7 was built in time for the 1974 Silverstone International Trophy where it was raced by Mike Hailwood in Yardley colours. Its career was confined to just five Grands Prix with the 'B team' before it was crashed heavily by Hailwood at the Nürburgring. The accident ended Mike's four-wheel racing career, and the car was virtually destroyed, leaving it as the only M23 controversially no longer accessible. The wrecked tub was donated to the Brands Hatch safety and fire marshals for training.

When the Formula 5000 M25/1 was converted into a Formula 1 car it was sometimes, erroneously, referred to in the press as 'M23/7'.

ABOVE TOP: No, it's not James Hunt but Scott Walker racing M23/6 in 2011. The Nürburgring is also hardly the same as Hunt would have known it. *(Jon Bunston)*

ABOVE: M23/7 on its last appearance; practice for the German Grand Prix 1974. *(Ford)*

ABOVE: M23/8
on Joaquin Folch-
Rusiñol's estate near
Barcelona. (Author)

Eventually, it was returned to the UK via Jeff Irwin, then a part-owner of Munich Legends, and subsequently sold to David Clark. Clark resold it to Joaquin Folch-Rusiñol. Kumschick Racing runs the car, now known by its original name of M23/8, for the Spaniard.

M23/8-2

In theory M23/8-2 should have been M23/10 but it was hurriedly built in 1975 to replace M23/8 and inherited the write-off's carnets. It made its debut at the non-championship Swiss Grand Prix at Dijon. There just was not the time to create the relevant paperwork for this, 'so we stamped the chassis plate M23/8-2,' remembered Wybrott. This plate remained on the car for the rest of its racing life.

Fittipaldi used M23/8-2 for the tail end of the 1975 season. It was also the first M23 to be driven by James Hunt, who tested it at Silverstone that December. It became his regular mount for his 1976 World Championship-winning season, coming first in the Spanish, Dutch, Canadian and US Grands Prix.

It was used by Hunt in South America the following season and at the 1977 Brands Hatch Race of Champions, where it became the last factory M23 to win a race. It was also the car in which Gilles Villeneuve made his Grand Prix debut later that season at Silverstone, and then by Bruno Giacomelli. It was thus the last works-entered M23.

The story is that a mechanic then took the M23/8-2 chassis tag from the car. It was then sold by McLaren to Dr Earl Hartley in America, and left the country with a chassis tag saying that it was simply chassis 'M23/8'. Steve Earle recalled that he had the opportunity to buy it (the price then being $125,000), but it was purchased by Adrian Hamilton, sold to Swiss Albert Obrist and was restored by Kerry Adams. Formula 1 supremo Bernie Ecclestone later acquired Obrist's collection, including this M23.

The fact that the original M23/8 and this car have both been known as 'M23/8' has led to confusion. The now Ecclestone-owned car was the tenth M23 to be made and not the eighth, which is (see above) owned by Joaquin Folch-Rusiñol.

M23/8 ('M23/10')

Built in 1974 with modified suspension, M23/8 made its debut at the British Grand Prix, where it was driven by Emerson Fittipaldi, who used it for the rest of his World Championship-winning season.

It was taken over by Jochen Mass at the start of the following year, and it was the car in which he won the truncated Spanish Grand Prix. It was effectively written off by Mass when trying hard in practice for the German Grand Prix, and was rebuilt by Leo Wybrott as a Texaco show car with the chassis number M23/10. 'We could not call it M23/8 any more because we now had M23/8-2,' said Wybrott, who was, himself, to purchase it from Texaco 'after it had had four years of being left outside service stations'.

Wybrott subsequently rebuilt M23/10 into a running car with new suspension. It was then warehoused in the Donington Collection until sold in 1983 to Allen Schuman and shipped to the USA. It was next sold, about four years later, via Harley Cluxton, to Chuck Kendall, father of multi-Trans-Am champion Tommy. The car went back to Cluxton to be sold on to Porsche parts dealer and restorer Bill Perrone, who raced it in historic events. During the mid-1990s Perrone received a substantial package of documents about the car, along with what was apparently claimed to be the original chassis plate M23-8, which Perrone refitted to the car. The whereabouts of the now-redundant M23/10 chassis plate are unknown.

OPPOSITE: James
Hunt at Fuji in 1976
in M23/8-2 and about
to win the World
Championship. (Ford)

ABOVE: The
conditions at Fuji
were pretty appalling
the day Hunt won the
World Championship,
as can be seen in this
shot of Jochen Mass
in M23/9. (Ford)

M23/9

M23/9 was built for the start of the 1975
season, making its debut at Argentina with
Emerson Fittipaldi at the wheel. The Brazilian,
who raced it for most of that year, scored a
first-time-out victory for the car, also using it
to win at Silverstone. The car competed in 29
major races, 26 of them Grands Prix. James
Hunt had two non-championship wins in the

car, one at the Race of Champions at Brands
Hatch and the other at the International Trophy
race at Silverstone, both in 1976.

It was mainly used by Mass during 1976.
The German crashed the car in Buenos Aires at
the start of 1977 and it was retired at that time.
Leo Wybrott had the right front repaired and
used it as a running museum display. James
Hunt drove it as such at the Gunnar Nilsson
Memorial Day at Donington Park in 1979.

RIGHT: M23/11 has
a claim to fame as
being the car that
gave Nelson Piquet,
seen here in Austria,
his Grand Prix debut.
(Ford)

It was in the Brooklands Collection for many years before going to New York-based entrepreneur Greg Galdi, who bought it from Wybrott around the turn of the millennium. It was restored by Kerry Adams with an engine from Nicholson McLaren. Galdi has since raced it on a regular basis, including at the first ever event at Austin in 2012. During the August of that year it also went on display in the Racing Research Center at Watkins Glen. It is now maintained by Mark Wehrmann of Hauppauge, NY-based Wehrrmann Engineering.

M23/11

Because of the slow development of the M26, two new cars were built for the start of the 1977 season, M23/11 being Hunt's mount, although it became the team spare after just two races. It later went to BS Fabrications as a back-up car for M23/14. After the latter was sold to Melchester Racing, Brett Lunger tried unsuccessfully to qualify it at Long Beach before taking delayed delivery of a new M26. Later in the season it was entered for Grand Prix debutant Nelson Piquet. The novice Brazilian's ninth place at Monza was the last Grand Prix appearance of an M23.

During the next two years, Riccardo Zunino and new owner Dennis Leech made brief appearances with the car in the Aurora AFX British Formula 1 Championship.

Sports car racer Ernst Schuster then purchased it at auction for £17,000 and Kerry Adams restored it. Adams, who recalled that Schuster did not fit into the car too well, discovered that the fuel cells were rotten. At about this time Willie Green track-tested it for *Classic & Sportscar* magazine.

It was put into the Christie's auction at Monte Carlo and was sold for £450,000, a considerable profit. The new owner was a consortium headed by Count Zenon. Shortly afterwards the market collapsed and the group lost a considerable amount of money. It went to Jeff Irwin in 1996 and then, in 2008, via David Clarke to Scott Walker, before being sold over the weekend of the Goodwood Revival 2012 to Charles Nearburg. It is now looked after for Nearburg by WDK Motorsport in Stockbridge.

M23/12

M23/12 was also built for the start of the 1977 season as Mass's regular car, making its debut at Long Beach. American dealer Harley Cluxton purchased it from McLaren in 1978 after it had only done six races. At one point he considered rebuilding it into a Can-Am car. However, it was purchased in 1986 by Steve Earle, a major figure in the promotion of historic Formula 1 cars in the USA. Earle retained it for over a decade before selling it to compatriot Richard Griot in 2008. Griot raced it a couple of times shortly after purchase, but it has not been seen lately.

ABOVE: Steve Earle, driving M23/12, and unfamiliar in a dark blue helmet, leads Bill Perrone round the corkscrew at Laguna Seca. *(Tony Griffiths collection)*

M23/14

The 13th chassis, known as M23/14, was built as a brand new customer car for Bob Sparshott's BS Fabrications team in 1977 and raced by Brett Lunger. The BS team helped to build the car at the McLaren factory. The American also raced it in early 1978 Grands Prix before selling it to Melchester Racing for Tony Trimmer to contest non-World Championship events. Trimmer finished third in the particularly wet Silverstone International Trophy and also won the British Formula 1 Championship with the car in 1978. Gordon Smiley contested three rounds of that series with it the following year. It was later owned by Fred Cziska from San Francisco. It remains in the USA with the current owner Bob Baker, who also owns M23/3. It is raced, now back in Chesterfield colours, by Danny Baker in historic events.

M25/1

The F5000 M25/1 is included here as it was temporarily converted to Formula 1 specification and became, to all intents and purposes, an M23. The last F5000 officially to be built by the factory, the M25 was detailed by John Barnard from the M23 design. Unloved by the works, it was sold to Carlos Avalone, but it was the subject of legal disputes before at last becoming the property of former British Speed Hillclimb Champion, David Hepworth. Three years after it was built, the 'twitchy' M25 was entered for two Shellsport G8 Championship rounds, driven by Bob Evans. It finished second at Brands Hatch and then retired at Thruxton, after which the money ran out.

It was then acquired by Giuseppe Risi for Emilio de Villota to drive. The Chevrolet V8 engine was replaced by a Cosworth DFV to create a back-up for the team's M23/6. Much of the suspension was reworked to later M23 specification, and it became virtually a Grand Prix standard M23. In the main, de Villota raced it in the Aurora AFX Championship. However, he did try, unsuccessfully, to qualify it for the 1978 Spanish Grand Prix. Here, the press confusingly referred to it as M25/M23-1, and even M23/7, the car effectively written off by Hailwood at the Nürburgring. The M25 was eventually sold to David McLaughlin, became part of the Foulston collection and was raced by John Foulston before becoming the property of Abba Kogan. It was restored back to F5000 specification in the yellow ochre colours of the Hepworth Racing Organisation. However, it has

since been rebuilt yet again as a Grand Prix car.

Looking back, Gordon Coppuck is wistful about the car. 'What happened to the M25 was a sacrilege. None of us within the company was interested in the production cars, but it would have been very strong if somebody could have done something with it. Denny said it was so lovely to drive, with that big old Chevy engine.'

TOP: Family affair: John Foulston laps Mary Foulston's Lotus 72 in a 1987 race at Brands Hatch. *(Jeff Bloxham)*

ABOVE AND LEFT: M25/1 was restored to F5000-spec after being acquired by Abba Kogan, although it barely resembled the original. However, seen above at Hall and Hall in 2009, it is now back in de Villota's colours as an F1 car. *(Marcus Pye and Jeff Bloxham)*

'We set a goal of the Aurora British
Formula 1 Championship.'

Tony Trimmer
Melchester Racing McLaren M23 driver, 1978

(Jeff Bloxham)

Chapter Seven

The privateer's view

The McLaren M23 had a successful career in the hands of privateers outside of the World Championship. Two South African, plus the British and Australian 'Formula 1' titles fell to the car. Four independent teams also entered them for Grands Prix, and it was one of these that scored the M23's last international podium place at the 1978 Silverstone International Trophy.

The McLaren M23's Grand Prix career coincided with the twilight years of the privateers. It would not be long before a bureaucratic regulation would insist that all teams entering World Championship races had to manufacture their own cars. The private entries that had contributed so much to the story of Grand Prix racing would be banished forever. Four M23s (M23/2, M23/6, M23/11 and M23/14) were, on various occasions, entered privately for Grands Prix. However, only the latter was specifically built for an independent team.

The non-championship, international Formula 1 races that once proliferated in the calendar and also gave the private entries greater opportunities, were also coming to an end. The final year in which Silverstone's International Trophy featured an entry of Grand Prix drivers and cars was 1978, with a privateer M23 finishing on the podium. The Race of Champions at Brands Hatch had just two more years, 1979 and 1983, to run. (James Hunt won the International Trophy and twice came first in the Race of Champions with a factory M23.) There were, however, still plenty of Formula 1 cars looking for somewhere to race, which led to frantic Grands Prix qualifying and even pre-qualifying sessions for the lesser lights during the latter years of the M23. National 'Formula 1'

series also gave a chance for M23s to perform in South Africa, Australia and the UK.

The first M23 to be raced in private hands was M23/2. Yorkshire-born Dave Charlton replaced his Lotus 72 with the car, extending his South African Drivers' Championship wins to six consecutive years in 1974 and 1975. In the first of these two seasons he won the initial five races (and six races in total) before Jody Scheckter's brother Ian changed his troublesome Firestone tyres to Goodyears on his Lotus 72, and proved that Charlton again had a real rival for the title. The following season he won three races, two fewer than a now Tyrrell-mounted Scheckter, but took the title with greater consistency.

Charlton also entered the Lucky Strike-sponsored car for the South African Grands Prix during this period, finishing 19th and 14th respectively. M23/2 was then sold to John McCormack, who replaced the Cosworth DFV with an aluminium Leyland P76 V8 engine to compete in the Australian Drivers' Championship in 1976 and 1977, winning the title the second year before fitting enveloping bodywork and taking it to North America to compete in the Can-Am Challenge.

It was in 1977 that privately entered M23s first started to appear in European Grands Prix. In the vanguard were Emilio de Villota and Brett

Lunger, whose M23s became regulars on the scene, although the Spanish journeyman, with airline and then banking sponsorship, failed to qualify more often than not. Lunger continued into the following season with his BS Fabrications car. This car also gave future World Champion Nelson Piquet his first three Grand Prix drives later in the year. Finally, Tony Trimmer, forced to use impossibly hard tyres, failed to qualify his Melchester Racing M23 for the 1978 British Grand Prix.

Trimmer and de Villota both contested the British Formula 1 series in 1978, with the Englishman winning the title. (De Villota used the converted M25/1 more than M23/6 during these races, while Davina Galica stood in for Trimmer on one occasion.) Both the BS and Melchester cars made sporadic appearances in 1979, driven by Gordon Smiley, Riccardo Zunino and Dennis Leech, and the last time two M23s appeared together on a contemporary grid was at Thruxton that May. The final contest for an M23 prior to their reappearance in historic racing was in October 1980 when saloon-car-driver Leech used M23/11, which he had now acquired from BS, to finish 11th. The McLaren M23 was amongst the last of a long line of Formula 1 cars that had served the privateer well.

TOP: **Emilio de Villota campaigned an M23 and the M25, and took in both Grands Prix and…** *(Ford)*

ABOVE: **…the Aurora British Formula 1 Championship. He is seen here at Oulton Park in 1978.** *(Jeff Bloxham)*

LEFT: **Gordon Smiley, who had two drives in the Melchester M23 in 1979, was killed in a horrific accident during qualifying for the Indianapolis 500 three years later.** *(Jeff Bloxham)*

Bob Sparshott and John Woodington (BS Fabrications)

Mechanic Bob Sparshott left Team Lotus in 1968, establishing his own company and returning to Formula 1 to run Mike Beuttler's Marches in the early 1970s. The association with March proved lucrative as he started fabricating parts for the fledgling race car manufacturer. The company became known as BS Fabrications, and Sparshott was joined by John Woodington as a fellow director. BS also built the Heskeths, which were to bring James Hunt to the fore, in a hat factory in Luton and, in 1976, ran a Surtees with Henri Pescarolo. By this stage it was also making parts for McLaren.

BS was based in Craddock Road, Luton (its third premises) by the time it ran its first M23 in 1977. It had arranged to prepare the McLaren for American Brett Lunger. Woodington, better known as 'Ace', recalled that the car (M23/14) could not be delivered on time, so they started the season with a March for Lunger, who brought with him sponsorship money from North American cigarette manufacturer Liggett & Myers. The company had different brands in different markets, so the car's livery had to be altered to suit.

'Teddy Mayer said the only way he would do this deal is if we did not harass them for parts. He was happy for us to make all of our own parts from their drawings,' recalled Sparshott. 'He knew we would make them correctly.'

Towards the end of the season, Lunger

decided that he wanted a spare car, so a second-hand M23 (M23/11) was purchased from the factory. The following year the team acquired an M26, so M23/14 was sold to Melchester Racing and M23/11 retained as a back-up. Lunger, who Sparshott and Woodington had run in Formula 2 back in 1972, was not short of money, for his mother was a DuPont. 'We did ask her for DuPont sponsorship,' recalled Woodington, but it didn't happen.

'Brett was brave, but he couldn't set a car up. We had to get him angry to qualify. When we signed Nelson Piquet to drive our other car, that annoyed him to the point where he started qualifying again,' said Woodington. Sparshott added that Lunger was only fast on his favourite, quicker circuits, like Silverstone and Spa. (Lunger is perhaps best known for his part in helping to rescue Niki Lauda from his Ferrari at the Nürburgring in 1976.)

The BS team had an illustrious line-up, with Dave Sims as team manager, Alan Jakeman as chief mechanic and Dave Pollard as engineer. Included amongst the mechanics was Paul Simpson who was to become Ayrton Senna's chief mechanic. The 'go-fer' was one Johnny Dumfries, now the Seventh Marquis of Bute and a one-time Lotus Grand Prix driver.

In 1978, BS gave future three-times World Champion Nelson Piquet his first Grand Prix drive. 'When he first drove the car he was shattered,' said Sparshott. 'He complained that the steering was very heavy. Once he threw it into the weeds because his arms were too tired. Racing drivers weren't very fit in those days! He had a sense of humour, though. During testing, a mechanic left a hammer in the foot well of

the car. The next day, when the dustsheet was removed, the seat was found to be full of hammers.'

'You can blame [Marlboro's] John Hogan for getting us to put Piquet in the car,' said Woodington. 'Lunger's sponsor, Liggett & Myers, had been bought by Marlboro. We were summoned to Hogan's office and told to take Lunger out. We said we couldn't do that, so Hogan said the second best thing would be for us to put Piquet in our other car. [By this time Lunger was driving an M26 but the team still had one of its M23s.] Bob and I went into the Formula 3 paddock and asked the first person we recognised where Piquet was. When we found him we simply asked if he would like to drive a Formula 1 car, and he said "yes". We gave him a business card and told him to be at our factory by 10am the next day for a seat fitting. We got him to sign a three-year contract with lots of let-out clauses. After Monza, Bernie [Ecclestone] said he wanted to buy out Piquet's contract. I should have put another nought on the figure we agreed!'

Sparshott remembered, 'He had already won the Formula 3 championship when we approached him at Brands Hatch, thinking that he must have already signed for someone else. What we hadn't realised was that Bernie was his mentor.

'When we got to Austria, the lads said, "Lunger's looking for you and he's not happy!" He accused me of using his sponsorship money "to run this kid", but I told him he could not be

more wrong. He was very upset, but I hadn't the heart to tell him he wasn't good enough. It had a good effect; he went even better than ever in practice for Austria.

'It poured with rain on the opening lap. Alan Jones later told me that Piquet had gone past him going up the hill as if he were standing still. Nelson hit the curb, although he hadn't realised it. They stopped the race and he came round. I saw the chassis was almost dragging on the ground. The front wheels had hit the curb so hard that the rockers had been bent. Nelson was sitting in there ready to go. I had to tell him he wasn't going anywhere.

'After the first-lap accident at Monza in 1978 when Ronnie Peterson was fatally injured, Lunger was understandably shaken up.' Piquet, by contrast was all ready to go out again. 'He was banging his heels up and down until he dented the bottom of the car. He simply asked me when the race was going to start. He had shut the accident out of his mind.'

'The M23 was a beautiful car; a privateer owner's dream car to run,' recalled Sparshott. 'That car was designed with maintenance in mind, the total reversal of a Lotus, where maintenance took second place to performance. It was a very sturdy, robust car, certainly not the lightest of monocoques.

'Because we used to make all the aluminium aerofoils for McLaren, we were sort of in control of our own destiny in that area. Engine changes were also quick to do. The air starter motor was fabulous. It all worked well;

THE NIGHTMARE

'The 1978 season was when we had to do pre-qualifying. That was a nightmare,' said Bob Sparshott. 'Bernie [Ecclestone] called a meeting at the Post House, Heathrow, as there was an unprecedented number of new teams. I think a lot of the foreign teams thought it was going to be a 'welcome to Formula 1' meeting. I remember his opening words: "Good afternoon ladies and gentlemen. I have to say that Formula 1 does not need you."

'Then we were told they would not have garages, would be working on the grass and would have to take part in a pre-qualifying session to see who went forward to qualifying. What he did not say at the time was that this would be on a different date. The demand on a team like us was incredible and it used to come down to the wire whether you made it or not. At one race we had failed to pre-qualify, had gone home and taken the car to pieces. We got a phone call to say that a driver who did not have to qualify was unable to start because of fuel burns. We were the next up; this was the Tuesday and we had to be back by Thursday… and we did it!'

the car was properly built with no short cuts.

'It was strong in the leg box area, which the drivers liked, of course, and that was proven in the Monza first-lap accident in 1978. Brett was involved and the car quite badly damaged, but he got away without any serious leg problems. The M23 obviously had a lot of input from the lads on the shop floor. Gordon Coppuck was a pretty practical bloke, anyway.'

When the rules stating that teams had to build their own cars came in, Sparshott and Woodington took the decision to cease being a Grand Prix entrant, although the company was to go on to win the inaugural Formula 3000 championship in 1985. It was not that BS wasn't capable of building its own car. It had made the Hesketh Formula 1 and early Toleman Formula 2 cars and was to construct the Indianapolis 500-winning Chaparral.

M23/11 was eventually sold for £6,000 to saloon-car driver Dennis Leech, 'who was about six foot six,' remembered Sparshott. 'He said he wasn't sure he could get in it, but "Ace" said, "You'll be all right", and was pushing him down.

'You try getting Dennis into an M23,' challenged Woodington. 'We persuaded him to cut the toes of his shoes off, but he still had to sit in the car with no seat, and it shook him to pieces.'

Tony Trimmer (Melchester Racing)

'We got the M23 just in time for the 1978 International Trophy at Silverstone,' recalled former Monaco Formula 3 winner and Lotus factory driver, Tony Trimmer. 'It was an ex-Brett Lunger car. Having won the Shellsport Group 8 Championship in 1977 with a Surtees TS19, we then moved to the McLaren. The first time I drove it was in qualifying for the International Trophy. Apart from that I had only sat in it. It turned out to be a very [Trimmer, understandably, repeats the word many times] wet race. I don't know how many times I spun at Abbey; I could not find a way round the bend. I spun, carried on, spun, carried on, spun and carried on. It was just untrue. By keeping going I finished the race third behind Keke Rosberg and Emerson Fittipaldi. They were lapping me just at the end so I followed them round on the slowing down lap and found out that they were cutting out Abbey altogether and going across the grass. I hadn't thought of that; it's probably too late to protest now.

'We then set a goal of the Aurora British Formula 1 Championship with Melchester Racing and Alan Charles as mechanic. I also helped on the car during the week. Melchester Racing was formed by Brian Morris, who owned a cleaning company and had encouraged some customers, who just happened to be Arab princes, to put finance in the team. The name combined Morris's home address and that of his company's office, Melbourne Close and Chester Place. After winning the Group 8 championship in 1977 with a Surtees, Brian and I had a discussion abut which car we would like to run the following year. I said that the McLaren M23 has such a good record and one of Brett Lunger's cars was up for sale. Brian agreed and we went for that. We maintained it in the old pit garages at Brands Hatch.'

In addition to racing in the Aurora series, Trimmer attempted to qualify the M23 for the British Grand Prix at Brands Hatch in 1978.

'The British Grand Prix was a disaster,' he recalled. He was forced to use an unsuitable set of particularly hard tyres in qualifying. 'I have never driven a car in such a bad state. I spun

LEFT: Tony Trimmer, seen here at Thruxton, retained the British Formula 1 title with the Melchester M23. *(Jeff Bloxham)*

on every corner, it was thoroughly dangerous.' Trimmer was not even allowed to use the lower specification tyres normally fitted for the Aurora series. 'Using them, I had done a lap at Brands during an earlier British Formula 1 Championship race that would have put me on the grid for the Grand Prix… and we had called those wooden tyres! It put something of a nail into my career because I had to explain to people every time just what had happened.

'We had pretty healthy and competitive grids for the 1978 Aurora series. The cars were identical to the current Grand Prix cars, but on fixed tyres that lasted for quite a few tests and races. That didn't matter, it kept the costs down and you could get a good balance on the car. We totalled five wins that year and weren't placed any lower than third in all races we finished. We had no problems with our two engines, which were prepared by Langford Peck and looked after by Bruce Stevens.

'Having won two series in two years, Melchester was approached by a number of people who wanted to be run by them. The Arabs had dropped out, but other drivers now wanted to bring their money into the team. I had to stand down.'

BELOW: The M23's final international podium came as a result of the farcical 1978 International Trophy at Silverstone. *Autosport* described Tony Trimmer's M23 as 'well driven' that day, but the result did come about as the leading drivers of the day seemed to spin off during the early laps. Towards the end of the particularly wet race, with hardly any cars left, the organisers dithered as to how many laps would be run before it was stopped. In the end it went the full distance and finished with the strangest of results, novice Keke Rosberg in a Theodore, of all things, winning ahead of former M23 man Emerson Fittipaldi in his Fittipaldi and, three laps back, two of the three M23s entered. (LAT)

OUT OF FORMULA 1

Chassis M23/2 had, arguably, the strangest career of all the cars. The 1973 British Grand Prix winner was the only one to race with other than a Cosworth DFV engine, competing with a V8 Leyland engine in both Formula 5000 and Can-Am events.

The driving force behind this was former double New Zealand Grand Prix-winner John McCormack who had been successfully campaigning Elfin F5000 cars in the Tasman Series and the Australian Drivers' Championship. He had been using Repco-Holden engines but, with rival Frank Matich being backed by the Repco works with the latest, free engines, he decided to look elsewhere for his power units. He tried to set up a deal before designer Phil Irving suggested during a dinner conversation that he look at the V8 engine Leyland had developed from the Buick/Rover V8 and which it was using in its large P76 saloon, having stoked it out to 4.4 litres. A meeting followed with Leyland Australia managing director Peter North, who expressed an interest in seeing the engine developed at a professional level. Irving agreed that the work could be done at Repco. A deal was done whereby engines would be supplied for exclusive use in Elfin factory cars.

A car was built, but there were some initial reliability problems. The engine was replaced by a Repco Holden and McCormack went on to win the Australian Drivers' Championship. 'However, the Leyland,' he said, 'was still unfinished business.'

It was now that a friend suggested he buy a McLaren M23 that was languishing in South Africa, where the local regulations had just changed from Formula 1 to Formula Atlantic. McCormack thus made contact with Dave Charlton, who had won the South African Formula 1 Championship with it in 1974 and 1975. A deal was done for the chassis alone, and the car landed in Australia for what McCormack recalled as Aus$12,000. Led by Dale Koenecke and Simon Aram, work began to convert it to a Formula 5000. 'I didn't want to bastardise the car, though,' said McCormack. However, removing the oil tank from its standard position gave sufficient room for the camshaft drive and accessory drive belts. The seat fuel tank was also removed to give space for the repositioned oil tank and the electric fuel pumps. Aram also designed a sub-frame structure, two supporting frames that McCormack still has to this day. Unlike the DFV, the Leyland V8 could not be used as a stressed member, and so Aram had to design a structure that would support both engine and transmission.

Repco produced one engine, but then, remembered McCormack, 'the global fuel crisis hit us. "V8" became a dirty word.' Repco ceased all involvement in F5000, and the Leyland P76 project was passed on to McCormack himself. 'Unfortunately, I never had enough money to pay for testing, so that had to be done at the race meetings, and the engine gained a reputation for unreliability.'

The car first appeared in its new guise to run in the Australian Drivers' Championship, the Gold Star, in late 1976, winning one race at Calder Park. The following year, McCormack was able to take the four-race series amassing 19 points with a win at Surfers Paradise, plus a second and a third. The following year he finished second in the championship with, again, one race win, this time at Oran Park, while he also put the M23 on pole for the Australian Grand Prix at Sandown.

In 1978, James Hunt was brought to Australia for a one-off drive in an Elfin at Winton Raceway.

RIGHT: Charlton's M23 went 'Down Under' sans engine. John McCormack installed a Leyland V8 and, like Charlton, took his national 'Formula 1' title. *(Stewart Clark)*

The Englishman was quickest in practice, but McCormack was beside him on the grid. A stone became jammed in the left rear brake, meaning John had to pit at the end of the first lap. However, back in the race he was able to record a fastest lap one-tenth of a second less than that of the former World Champion.

F5000, by this time, was falling out of favour in Australia, and McCormack decided if he wanted to continue making a living as a racing driver he would have to go to North America and compete in the Can-Am Championship. By this time the series was no longer for the type of big sports car, such as had been run in the days when the series was dominated by Bruce McLaren and Denny Hulme. The cars still had enveloping bodywork, but featured central seats, meaning that many of them were converted open wheelers. McCormack planned to convert the M23, do two or three races, and then try to get a drive with another team. 'With hindsight, I should have just bought a drive,' he later said. A couple of single plane crankshafts were made to take the engine back to four-litres as specified by the regulations, while Aram fitted a sports-car body. When doing this work, the team was able to note where the car had been repaired following Scheckter's crash when he had raced it in North America. A double-deck trailer was built, and sponsorship was found with a shipping line before team and family set off for the USA.

Looking like no other M23 before or since, M23/2 was raced three times in the States. The engine gave out after only a couple of laps at Mosport, 'but they still gave me 600 bucks'. Overheating caused the car to retire at Mid-Ohio, and then it was classified 12th at Watkins Glen.

McCormack now returned to Australia to race a Jaguar XJS in the colours of car components supplier Unipart, which had backed the M23 during his second season with the car. The Australian Grand Prix in those days was still a local affair, nothing to do with the World Championship. However, in 1980, the newly crowned champion Alan Jones was entered in a Williams alongside Bruno Giacomelli in a factory Alfa Romeo. The rest of the field were, mainly, local F5000s. Unipart Australia managing director John Shingleton asked, if he could get some money together, would McCormack consider running the McLaren again? The car had to be returned to single-seater trim, the opportunity being taken to get the weight down from 1,420lb to 1,260lb by getting rid of such as the airbox and starter motor, and by replacing the battery with two small, Yuasa motorcycle ones, which only had to run the fuel pump and the ignition. The one-mile Calder circuit had three right-hand bends and just one left-hand bend, so McCormack also took a leaf out of the IndyCar book by putting stagger on to the car.

The event was a week-long promotion, with shakedown scheduled for the Sunday before the race. The track was 465 miles from McCormack's base. Normally he would have flown, but because of an airline refuellers' strike he went as passenger in a car belonging to one of his crew. There was plenty of fog about that day, and McCormack had told the mechanic to keep well back from the transporter that led them on the road. About 150 miles out, the mechanic must have dozed off, the car crashed and hit a tree, and the pair suffered serious injuries. That, to McCormack's head, effectively meant the end of his racing career.

McCormack moved to Tasmania, taking the M23, and a considerable amount of spares, with him. 'Out of the blue' Leo Wybrott contacted him to see if it was for sale. At first they could not agree a price, but a year later Wybrott approached him again and a deal was struck, whereby the car returned to McLaren.

Many years later, McCormack was at Silverstone for an historic car event. Standing outside the Hall and Hall area in the paddock he noticed an M23 nose in Unipart colours. Although the car had by now passed into the hands of Jody Scheckter, it appeared that McLaren had held on to the nose, which had eventually been sold to Hall and Hall so that it could create a mould for the M23 it was running for Scott Walker.

ABOVE: The strangest guise in which an M23 appeared. The enveloping body fitted by McCormack to comply with the then Can-Am Challenge rules that had been changed to permit centrally seated cars. *(Wayne Ellwood)*

Epilogue

It was simple, it was straightforward, it became innovative and it won two World Championships. What more can one ask? McLaren has taken 12 World Driver's Championships and eight Constructors' titles, but it was the M23 that the first of these fell to in 1974.

The McLaren M23 contested Grands Prix over six long years (although only in privateer hands in its final season), an inordinate length of time for a Formula 1 car. As designer Gordon Coppuck was reported to have said towards the end of its career, McLaren expected to build a car for a two-year racing life, the first to sort it out, and the second for it to be competitive. A third year was a bonus. The M23 certainly won the World Championship in its second year... but it took it again in its fourth.

Between them, the McLaren M23 and the Lotus 72 defined Formula 1 in the early to mid-1970s, with the Lotus outscoring its slightly later rival with 20 wins from 75 Grand Prix starts to 16 from 83. However, the M23, unlike the Lotus, was quick out of the box and remained relatively competitive throughout its life. Both were driven to World Championship victory by two drivers, Emerson Fittipaldi being a common denominator.

To appear truly great in the eyes of history, a racing car ideally needs to have gone mano-a-mano with a worthy rival; in 1976 the McLaren M23 did just that. It was M23 versus Ferrari 312T2. True, the McLaren had won the championship before in 1974, but that season just did not have the same drama, even if it did go down to the proverbial wire; you cannot imagine Ron Howard directing a film about it.

There is a case to make that the McLaren was more the villain than the hero of the piece. The repositioning of the oil coolers and the temporary disqualification for being too wide indicate that. Add to this the argument that, in all the twists and turns, the disqualifications and the reinstatements, the major deciding factor in the destination of the championship was Lauda's horrific accident at the Nürburgring. Nevertheless, it should be remembered that the M23 was, by then, in its fourth active year and its final complete one as the factory's main weapon. Despite this venerable quality, it was still good enough to enable James Hunt to overcome the vagaries of the season and to take advantage of the way the dice fell.

Appendices

McLaren M23 specification (1973)

Chassis
Deformable double-skinned aluminium monocoque.
Body: Monocoque lower, GRP nose, cockpit and engine cover.
Front suspension: Tubular upper rocker arm, operating inboard coil spring/damper, lower wishbone, anti-roll bar.
Rear suspension: Adjustable top link, reverse lower wishbone, twin radius rods, coil spring/damper, anti-roll bar.
Brakes front/rear: Outboard/inboard ventilated discs.

Wheel diameter and width
   front/rear: 13 x 11in/13 x 18in.

Engine
Type: Cosworth DFV.
Capacity: 2,993cc.
Bore and stroke: 85.6mm x 64.8mm.
Compression ratio: 11:1.
Maximum power and rpm: 460bhp at 10,000rpm.
Valves Inlet: 1.32in x 2.
          Outlet: 1.14in x 2.
Valve lift: 0.4in.
Valve timings: 62, 86, 86, 62.
Fuel system: Lucas fuel injection.

Transmission
Gearbox: Hewland FG400 5sp.

Dimensions
Wheelbase: 101in.
Track: 65.5in front, 62.5in rear.
Length: 170in.
Width: 80in.
Height of airbox: 46in.
Weight: 1,270lb.

Changes
1974
Wheelbase: 104.2in.
Track: 64.2in front, 66in rear.
Length: 165in.
Height of airbox: 48in.

1975
Brakes: 13 x 10in/13 x 18in.
Power output: 465bhp.
Rear suspension: Adjustable top link, parallel lower links, twin radius rods, coil spring/damper, anti-roll bar.
Wheelbase: 105.75in.
Track: 64.2in front, 65in rear.
Length: 167in.
Width: 82in.
Height of airbox: 49in.
Weight: 1,325lb.
1976
Height: 36in.
Wheelbase: 107in.
Weight: 1,295lb.

McLaren M23 and M25 World Championship Grand Prix history

1973		
3 March	South African GP – Kyalami	5th Denny Hulme M23/1
29 April	Spanish GP – Montjuich Park	4th Peter Revson M23/2 • 5th Hulme M23/1
20 May	Belgian GP – Zolder	7th Hulme M23/1 • Rtd Revson M23/2
3 June	Monaco GP – Monte Carlo	5th Revson M23/2 • 6th Hulme M23/1
17 June	Swedish GP – Anderstorp	1st Hulme M23/1 • 7th Revson M23/2
1 July	French GP – Paul Ricard	8th Hulme M23/1 • Rtd Jody Scheckter M23/3
14 July	British GP – Silverstone	1st Revson M23/2 • 3rd Hulme M23/1 • Rtd Scheckter M23/3
29 July	Dutch GP – Zandvoort	4th Revson M23/2 • Rtd Hulme M23/1
5 August	German GP – Nürburgring	3rd Jacky Ickx M23/4 • 9th Revson M23/2 • 12th Hulme M23/1
19 August	Austrian GP – Österreichring	8th Hulme M23/1 • Rtd Revson M23/2
9 September	Italian GP – Monza	3rd Revson M23/4 • 15th Hulme M23/1
23 September	Canadian GP – Mosport	1st Revson M23/4 • 13th Hulme M23/1 • Rtd Scheckter M23/2
7 October	US GP – Watkins Glen	4th Hulme M23/1 • 5th Revson M23/4 • Rtd Scheckter M23/2
1974		
13 January	Argentine GP – Buenos Aires	1st Hulme M23/6 • 4th Mike Hailwood M23/1 • 10th Emerson Fittipaldi M23/5
27 January	Brazilian GP – Interlagos	1st Fittipaldi M23/5 • 5th Hailwood M23/1 • 12th Hulme M23/6
30 March	South African GP – Kyalami	3rd Hailwood M23/1 • 7th Fittipaldi M23/5 • 9th Hulme M23/6 • 19th Dave Charlton M23/2
28 April	Spanish GP – Jarama	3rd Fittipaldi M23/5 • 6th Hulme M23/4 • 9th Hailwood M23/7
12 May	Belgian GP Nivelles – Baulers	1st Fittipaldi M23/5 • 6th Hulme M23/6 • 7th Hailwood M23/7
26 May	Monaco GP – Monte Carlo	5th Fittipaldi M23/5 • Rtd Hailwood M23/1 • Rtd Hulme M23/6
9 June	Swedish GP – Anderstorp	4th Fittipaldi M23/4 • Rtd Hailwood M23/7 • Rtd Hulme M23/6
23 June	Dutch GP – Zandvoort	3rd Fittipaldi M23/5 • 4th Hailwood M23/7 • Rtd Hulme M23/6
7 July	French GP – Dijon-Prenois	6th Hulme M23/6 • 7th Hailwood M23/7 • Rtd Fittipaldi M23/5

DNQ	Did not qualify
DNS	Did not start
DSQ	Disqualified
NC	Not classified
Rtd	Retired
Wdn	Withdrawn

20 July	*British GP – Brands Hatch*	2nd Fittipaldi M23/8 • 7th Hulme M23/6 • Rtd Hailwood M23/1
4 August	*German GP – Nürburgring*	15th Hailwood M23/7 • Rtd Fittipaldi M23/8 • Rtd Hulme M23/6
18 August	*Austrian GP – Österreichring*	2nd Hulme M23/6 • 7th David Hobbs M23/4 • Rtd Fittipaldi M23/8
8 September	*Italian GP – Monza*	2nd Fittipaldi M23/8 • 6th Hulme M23/6 • 9th Hobbs M23/4
22 September	*Canadian GP – Mosport*	5th Fittipaldi M23/8 • 6th Hulme M23/6 • 16th Jochen Mass M23/4
6 October	*US GP – Watkins Glen*	4th Fittipaldi M23/8 • 7th Mass M23/4 • Rtd Hulme M23/6
1975		
12 January	*Argentine GP – Buenos Aires*	1st Fittipaldi M23/9 • 14th Mass M23/8
26 January	*Brazilian GP – Interlagos*	2nd Fittipaldi M23/9 • 3rd Mass M23/8
1 March	*South African GP – Kyalami*	6th Mass M23/8 • 14th Charlton M23/2 • Rtd Fittipaldi M23/6
27 April	*Spanish GP – Montjuich Park*	1st Mass M23/8 • DNS Fittipaldi M23/9
11 May	*Monaco GP – Monte Carlo*	2nd Fittipaldi M23/9 • 6th Mass M23/6
25 May	*Belgian GP – Zolder*	7th Fittipaldi M23/9 • Rtd Mass M23/8
8 June	*Swedish GP – Anderstorp*	8th Fittipaldi M23/9 • Rtd Mass M23/8
22 June	*Dutch GP – Zandvoort*	Rtd Fittipaldi M23/9 • Rtd Mass M23/8
6 July	*French GP – Paul Ricard*	3rd Mass M23/9 • 4th Fittipaldi M23/8
19 July	*British GP – Silverstone*	1st Fittipaldi M23/9 • 7th Mass M23/8
3 August	*German GP – Nürburgring*	Rtd Fittipaldi M23/9 • Rtd Mass M23/8
17 August	*Austrian GP – Österreichring*	4th Mass M23/6 • 9th Fittipaldi M23/9
7 September	*Italian GP – Monza*	2nd Fittipaldi M23/8-2 • Rtd Mass M23/6
5 October	*US GP – Watkins Glen*	2nd Fittipaldi M23/8-2 • 3rd Mass M23/6
1976		
25 January	*Brazilian GP – Interlagos*	6th Mass M23/6 • Rtd Hunt M23/8-2
6 March	*South African GP – Kyalami*	2nd Hunt M23/8-2 • 3rd Mass M23/6
28 March	*US (West) GP – Long Beach*	5th Mass M23/6 • Rtd Hunt M23/8-2
2 May	*Spanish GP – Jarama*	1st Hunt M23/8-2 • Rtd Mass M23/9
16 May	*Belgian GP – Zolder*	6th Mass M23/9 • Rtd Hunt M23/6
30 May	*Monaco GP – Monte Carlo*	5th Mass M23/9 • Rtd Hunt M23/8-2
13 June	*Swedish GP – Anderstorp*	4th Hunt M23/6 • 11th Mass M23/9
4 July	*French GP – Paul Ricard*	1st Hunt M23/6 • 15th Mass M23/9
18 July	*British GP – Brands Hatch*	Rtd Mass M23/9 • DSQ Hunt M23/6
1 August	*German GP – Nürburgring*	1st Hunt M23/6 • 3rd Mass M23/9
15 August	*Austrian GP – Österreichring*	4th Hunt M23/6 • 7th Mass M23/9
29 August	*Dutch GP – Zandvoort*	1st Hunt M23/8-2
12 September	*Italian GP – Monza*	Rtd Hunt M23/8-2 • Rtd Mass M23/6
3 October	*Canadian GP – Mosport*	1st Hunt M23/8-2 • 5th Mass M23/9
10 October	*US (East) GP – Watkins Glen*	1st Hunt M23/8-2 • 4th Mass M23/9
24 October	*Japanese GP – Fuji*	3rd Hunt M23/8-2 • Rtd Mass M23/9
1977		
9 January	*Argentine GP – Buenos Aires*	Rtd Hunt M23/8-2 • Rtd Mass M23/9
23 January	*Brazilian GP – Interlagos*	2nd Hunt M23/8-2 • Rtd Mass M23/9
5 March	*South African GP – Kyalami*	4th Hunt M23/11 • 5th Mass M23/6
3 April	*US (West) GP – Long Beach*	7th Hunt M23/11 • Rtd Mass M23/12
8 May	*Spanish GP – Jarama*	4th Mass M23/12 • 13th Emilio de Villota M23/6
22 May	*Monaco GP – Monte Carlo*	4th Mass M23/12 • Rtd Hunt M23/8
5 June	*Belgian GP – Zolder*	Ret Mass M23/12 • DNQ de Villota M23/6 • DNS Brett Lunger M23/14
19 June	*Swedish GP – Anderstorp*	2nd Mass M23/12 • 11th Lunger M23/14 • DNQ de Villota M23/6
3 July	*French GP – Dijon-Prenois*	9th Mass M23/12 • DNQ Lunger M23/14
16 July	*British GP – Silverstone*	11th Gilles Villeneuve M23/8-2 • 13th Lunger M23/14 • DNQ de Villota M23/6
31 July	*German GP – Hockenheim*	Rtd Lunger M23/14 • DNQ de Villota M23/6
14 August	*Austrian GP – Österreichring*	10th Lunger M23/14 • 17th de Villota M23/6
28 August	*Dutch GP – Zandvoort*	9th Lunger M23/14
11 September	*Italian GP – Monza*	Rtd Bruno Giacomelli M23/8-2 • Rtd Lunger M23/14 • DNQ de Villota M23/6
2 October	*US (East) GP – Watkins Glen*	10th Lunger M23/14
9 October	*Canadian GP – Mosport*	11th Lunger M23/14

1978		
15 January	*Argentine GP – Buenos Aires*	13th Lunger M23/14
29 January	*Brazilian GP – Rio de Janeiro*	Rtd Lunger M23/14
4 March	*South African GP – Kyalami*	11th Lunger M23/14
2 April	*US (West) GP – Long Beach*	DNQ Lunger M23/11
4 June	*Spanish GP – Jarama*	DNQ de Villota M25/1
16 July	*British GP – Brands Hatch*	DNQ Tony Trimmer M23/14
13 August	*Austrian GP – Österreichring*	Rtd Nelson Piquet M23/11
27 August	*Dutch GP – Zandvoort*	Rtd Piquet M23/11
10 September	*Italian GP – Monza*	9th Piquet M23/11

Drivers' World Championship

1973 Peter Revson 5th 38 points (also M19)
Denny Hulme 6th 26 points (also M19)
Jacky Ickx 9th 12 points (also Ferrari and
also ISO-Williams)
Jody Scheckter – *did not score*.

1974 Emerson Fittipaldi 1st 55 points
Denny Hulme 7th 20 points
Mike Hailwood 11th 12 points
**Dave Charlton, David Hobbs and
Jochen Mass** – *did not score*.

1975 Emerson Fittipaldi 2nd 45 points
Jochen Mass 8th 20 points
Dave Charlton – did not score.

1976 James Hunt 1st 69 points
Jochen Mass 9th 19 points (also M26)

1977 James Hunt 5th 40 points
Jochen Mass 6th 25 points (also M26)
**Gilles Villeneuve, Bruno Giacomelli, Emilio de Villota
and Brett Lunger** – *did not score*.

1978 Brett Lunger, Nelson Piquet, Emilio de Villota and
Tony Trimmer – *did not score*.

Constructors' Championship

1973	3rd	58 points (also M19)
1974	1st	73 (75) points
1975	3rd	61 points
1976	2nd	74 (75) points
1977	3rd	60 points (also M26)
1978		0 points

McLaren M23 and M25 non-World Championship race history

1973		
18 March	*Race of Champions – Brands Hatch*	2nd Denny Hulme M23/1
8 April	*BRDC International Trophy – Silverstone*	4th Peter Revson M23/2 • Rtd Hulme M23/1
1974		
3 February	*Grande Premio Presidente Medici – Brasilia*	1st Emerson Fittipaldi M23/5
17 March	*Race of Champions – Brands Hatch*	3rd Fittipaldi M23/4 • 4th Mike Hailwood M23/1 • Rtd Hulme M23/6
7 April	*BRDC International Trophy – Silverstone*	Rtd Hailwood M23/7 • Rtd Hulme M23/4
13 April	*Mercury 100 – Roy Hesketh*	1st Dave Charlton M23/2
4 May	*Cape South Easter Trophy – Killarney*	1st Charlton M23/2
25 May	*South African Republic Trophy – Kyalami*	1st Charlton M23/2
15 June	*Brandkop Winter Trophy – Brandkop*	1st Charlton M23/2
30 June	*Bulawayo 100 – Bulawayo*	1st Charlton M23/2
13 July	*Natal Winter Trophy – Roy Hesketh*	2nd Charlton M23/2
10 August	*Rand Winter Trophy – Kyalami*	1st Charlton M23/2
31 August	*False Bay 100 – Killarney*	2nd Charlton M23/2
15 September	*Rhodesian GP – Donnybrook*	3rd Charlton M23/2
28 September	*Rand Spring Trophy – Kyalami*	2nd Charlton M23/2
19 October	*Goldfields 100 – Goldfields*	8th Charlton M23/2

1975		
8 February	*Cape South Easter Trophy – Killarney*	1st Charlton M23/2
16 March	*Race of Champions – Brands Hatch*	5th Fittipaldi M23/9 • Rtd Jochen Mass M23/8
22 March	*Goldfields 100 – Goldfields*	DSQ Charlton M23/2
29 March	*Natal Mercury 100 – Roy Hesketh*	2nd Charlton M23/2
13 April	*BRDC International Trophy – Silverstone*	2nd Fittipaldi M23/4
3 May	*Brandkorp Winter Trophy – Brandkorp*	2nd Charlton M23/2
31 May	*South African Republic Trophy – Kyalami*	2nd Charlton M23/2
5 July	*False Bay 100 – Killarney*	2nd Charlton M23/2
26 July	*Rand Winter Trophy – Kyalami*	2nd Charlton M23/2
24 August	*Swiss GP – Hockenheim*	3rd Mass M23/6 • Rtd Fittipaldi M23/8-2
1 September	*Natal Spring Trophy – Roy Hesketh*	1st Charlton M23/2
4 October	*Rand Spring Trophy – Kyalami*	2nd Charlton M23/2
1976		
14 March	*Race of Champions – Brands Hatch*	1st James Hunt M23/8
11 April	*BRDC International Trophy – Silverstone*	1st Hunt M23/9
1977		
20 March	*Race of Champions – Brands Hatch*	1st Hunt M23/8-2
16 October	*Shellsport G8 Championship round – Brands Hatch*	Rtd Emilio de Villota M25/1*
1978		
19 March	*BRDC International Trophy – Silverstone*	3rd Tony Trimmer M23/14 • 4th Brett Lunger M23/11 • Rtd de Villota M23/6
24 March	*International Gold Cup – Oulton Park*	1st Trimmer M23/14 • 2nd de Villota M25/1
27 March	*Evening News Trophy – Brands Hatch*	1st Trimmer M23/14 • 3rd de Villota M25/1
16 April	*Anglia TV Trophy – Snetterton*	1st Trimmer M23/14 • 2nd de Villota M25/1
1 May	*Sun Trophy – Mallory Park*	2nd Trimmer M23/14 • 4th de Villota M25/1
15 May	*International Whitsuntide – Zandvoort*	Rtd de Villota M25/1 • DNS Trimmer M23/14
21 May	*Donington Formula 1 Trophy – Donington Park*	5th de Villota M25/1
29 May	*Radio 210 European Trophy – Thruxton*	1st Trimmer M23/14
24 June	*Oulton Park Formula 1 Trophy – Oulton Park*	Rtd de Villota M23/6
30 July	*Dave Lee Travis Trophy – Mallory Park*	2nd Trimmer M23/14 • 4th de Villota M23/6
28 August	*Fuji Tapes Trophy – Brands Hatch*	1st Trimmer M23/14
10 September	*Radio Victory Trophy – Thruxton*	7th Davina Galica M23/14 • 8th de Villota M25/1
24 September	*Budweiser Trophy – Snetterton*	2nd Trimmer M23/14 • 8th de Villota M25/1
1979		
20 May	*Anglia TV Trophy – Snetterton*	7th Gordon Smiley M23/14
28 May	*Rivet Supply Trophy – Thruxton*	4th Smiley M23/14 • 5th Ricardo Zunino M23/11
4 June	*International Whitsuntide – Zandvoort*	5th Smiley M23/14
9 September	*Radio Victor Trophy – Thruxton*	9th Dennis Leech M23/11
1980		
5 October	*Pentax Trophy – Silverstone*	11th Leech M23/11

* Note that M25/1 also competed in the Shellsport G8 rounds at Brands Hatch and Thruxton on 30 August and 12 September respectively, driven by Bob Evans. However, it was still in its original F5000 specification, using a V8 Chevrolet engine. M23/3 was also campaigned in F5000 specification, with V8 Rover engine, in Australia in 1976 and 1977, John McCormack winning the Australian Drivers' Championship with it in the latter year.

South African Drivers' Championship

| 1974 | **Dave Charlton** | 1st | 67 points |
| 1975 | **Dave Charlton** | 1st | 54 points |

British Formula One Series

1978	**Tony Trimmer**	1st	149 points
	Emilio de Villota	3rd	86 points
	(also M25 and Boxer)		
1979	**Ricardo Zunino**	5th	39 points
	(also Arrows)		
	Gordon Smiley	9th	18 points
	(also Tyrrell and Surtees)		
	Dennis Leech – *did not score.*		

McLaren M23 and M25 F5000 and Can-Am race history

1976		
30 August	*Shellsport G8 Championship round – Brands Hatch*	2nd Bob Evans M25/1
11 September	*Australian Gold Star race –Sandown Park*	DNS John McCormack M23/2
12 September	*Shellsport G8 Championship round – Thruxton*	Rtd Evans M25/1
16 October	*Australian Gold Star race – Calder Park*	2nd McCormack M23/2
17 October	*Australian Gold Star race – Calder Park*	1st McCormack M23/2
13 November	*Australian Gold Star race – Phillip Island*	3rd McCormack M23/2
28 November	*Australian Gold Star race – Phillip Island*	5th McCormack M23/2
1977		
6 February	*Australian Grand Prix – Oran Park*	Rtd McCormack M23/2
13 February	*Surfers Paradise 100 – Surfers Paradise*	NC McCormack M23/2
20 February	*Sandown Park Cup – Sandown Park*	7th McCormack M23/2
27 February	*Adelaide 100 – Adelaide International*	6th McCormack M23/2
28 August	*Australian Gold Cup race – Surfers Paradise*	1st McCormack M23/2
11 September	*Australian Gold Cup race – Sandown Park*	Rtd McCormack M23/2
16 October	*Australian Gold Cup Race – Calder Raceway*	2nd McCormack M23/2
30 October	*Rose City 10,000 – Winton Raceway*	1st McCormack M23/2
13 November	*Australian Gold Cup race – Phillip Island*	3rd McCormack M23/2
1978		
12 February	*Adelaide 100 – Adelaide International*	DNS McCormack M23/2
19 February	*Surfers Paradise 100 – Surfers Paradise*	10th McCormack M23/2
26 February	*Oran Park 100 – Oran Park*	Rtd McCormack M23/2
30 July	*Australian Gold Star Race – Oran Park*	1st McCormack M23/2
10 September	*Australian Grand Prix – Sandown Park*	Rtd McCormack M23/2
15 October	*Australian Gold Star race – Calder Park*	4th McCormack M23/2
29 October	*Rose City 10,000 – Winton Raceway*	Rtd McCormack M23/2
1979		
4 February	*Sandown Park Cup – Sandown Park*	Rtd McCormack M23/2
11 February	*Adelaide 100 – Adelaide International*	Rtd McCormack M23/2
18 February	*Surfers Paradise 100 – Surfers Paradise*	DNS McCormack M23/2
25 February	*Oran Park 100 – Oran Park*	5th McCormack M23/2
11 March	*Australian Grand Prix – Wanneroo Park*	Rtd McCormack M23/2
3 June	*Can-Am Challenge race – Mosport Park*	Rtd McCormack M23/2
10 June	*Can-Am Challenge race – Mid-Ohio*	Rtd McCormack M23/2
8 July	*Can-Am Challenge race – Watkins Glen*	12th McCormack M23/2
1980		
16 November	*Australian Grand Prix – Calder Park*	DNA McCormack M23/2

Shellsport G8 Championship

1976   Bob Evans   21st   15 points

Rothmans International Series

1977   John McCormack   =9th   3 points

Australian National Formula One Championship

1976   John McCormack   3rd   11 points
1977   John McCormack   1st   19 points
1978   John McCormack   2nd   12 points

Can-Am Challenge

1979   John McCormack   –   Did not score

**Single-Seater Racing Cars –
International Formulae (Group 8).**

Art. 293. – Formula No. 1.

Validity: from the lst January 1966 to
31st December 1975.
Engines with reciprocating pistons:
a) engine cylinder-capacity without
   supercharging: inferior or equal to
   3,000cc;
b) engine cylinder-capacity with
   supercharging; inferior or equal to
   1,500cc.
Number of cylinders: max 12.
Turbine engine
Utilization authorized on the basis of the
Equivalence Formula given under
Art. 252 j).
Minimum weight, without ballast: 575kg.

Technical Regulations with effect from 1/1/73.

Overall body dimensions: the overall
maximum width behind the front wheels
to the loading edge of the rear wheels
shall not exceed 140cm. No oil, fuel and
electrical lines shall be situated beyond
60cm on either side of the car's centre
line and must not run adjacent to the
main fuel cells or within the crushable
structure.

The remainder of the present
regulation remains unchanged. Therefore
the maximum width of the rear wing
remains at 110cm.
Rubber bladder fuel cells: all fuel tanks
will be situated within the main structure
of the car.

All fuel tanks beyond 30cm on either
side of the car's centre line must be non-
self-sealing rubber bladders conforming
to the Specification hereafter. A tank
situated within the main monocoque not
extending beyond 30cm on the centre
line of the car must be FT3 material, or
the above material.

All tanks will be fitted with self-sealing
breakaway couplings (aviation type).

A collector tank of maximum one
gallon may be placed outside the main
chassis on condition that it be surrounded
by crushable structure conforming to
the specifications hereafter of at least
10mm thickness. The rubber bladder to
be to FT3 specifications. The fuel system
should be so arranged as no part of
it is the first object to be struck in an
accident.

Oil tanks: as from 1974, all oil storage
tanks, situated outside the main structure
of the car, must be surrounded by 10mm
thick crushable structure. In any case, no
oil storage tank, not located within the
main structure, may be situated
aft of the gearbox or final drive casing.
Fire extinguisher: for all cars, as from
1/1/74, the entire fire extinguishing
system must be located within the main
structure.
Crushable structure: the entire fuel tank
area of the car in direct contact with
the open airstream must incorporate a
crushable structure conforming to the
specification hereafter.
The term 'licked by the open air stream'
is considered to define the complete
external area of the body/monocoque
construction irrespective of such added
items as water radiators, inlet ducts,
windscreens, etc.
a) The crushable structure should be a
sandwich construction based on fire
resistant core of minimum crushing
strength of 25lb/square inch. It shall be
permitted to pass water pipes through
this core.

The sandwich construction must
include two sheets of 1.5mm thickness,
one of which shall be aluminium sheet
having a tensile strength of 14tons/square
inch and minimum elongation of 5%.
b) The minimum thickness of the
sandwich construction should be 10mm.
The fore and aft fuel tank area, however,
should provide for a crushable structure
of at least 100mm thickness at such
crushable structure's thickest point, the
position of this widest point to be at the
constructor's discretion, over a length
of at least 35cm, after which it may be
gradually reduced to 10mm.
Fuel capacity: the total capacity of the
fuel tanks shall not exceed 250 litres
of which not more than 80 litres shall
be contained in any one tank. (The fuel
system must be arranged not to allow
more than 80 litres of fuel to spill in the
event of a rupture of any one principal
fuel tank.)
Safety roll-bar: the safety roll-over bar
will have a minimum height of 82cm
(identical checking method as for the
height of wings on cars with bodywork).
In all cases, the top of the safety roll-over
bar will be at least 5cm above the helmet
of the driver.
**Implementation of the new
specifications:** the specifications
regarding maximum tank capacity must

be observed as from 1/1/1973. The
remaining
specifications must be complied with for
the first Grand Prix held in Europe in
1973.

However, cars built before 31/12/72
and raced during the 1972 season will be
allowed to use FIA/Spec/FT3 safety tanks.
All other safety measures will have
to be observed.

Art. 296. – Prescriptions and definitions applicable to racing cars of the 3 international formulae.

a) Minimum weight: the minimum weight
is that of the car in running order
i.e. with all lubrication and cooling liquids
but without fuel.

The ballast which is prohibited is
that of a removable type. It is therefore
permissible to complete the weight of
the car through one or several ballasts
incorporated to the materials of the car
provided that solid and unitary blocks are
used, and that they are fixed by means of
a tool and offer the opportunity of being
sealed on should the officials entrusted
with the scrutineering of the car deem it
necessary.
b) The construction of the vehicle must
be symmetrical i.e. when the car is lifted
laterally and weighed, the half weight
on either side must be equal to half the
overall weight, a margin of + or – 5%
being allowed for the said half weight.
To verify the above, the weighing must be
done with all tanks full (fuel, water, oil) and
a driver, weighing at least 75 kilos normally
sitting at the steering-wheel (or a ballast
of the same weight occupying the same
place).
c) Reverse gear: all vehicles must have
a gearbox including a reverse gear, which
must be in working order when the car
starts the events and able to be operated
by the driver when normally in his seat.
d) Compulsory automatic starter with
electrical or other source of energy carried
aboard the car and able to be controlled
by the driver when normally in his seat.
e) Driver's seat liable to be occupied or
left without it being necessary to open
a door or remove a panel. Sitting at his
steering-wheel the driver must be facing
the road. Moreover, the cockpit must be
so conceived that the maximum time
necessary for the driver to get in or out
does not exceed 5 seconds.

f) Safety harness: Cars must be equipped with a 'six-point' safety harness i.e. a harness made of two shoulder straps, one abdominal strap and two crutch straps. The wearing of this harness is compulsory.

g) Coachwork: No part of the coachwork, with the exception of the safety roll bar, shall exceed in height a horizontal plane, 80cm above the lowest point of the entirely sprung structure of the car.

In other words, a car with its wheels and the mobile suspension elements removed, but without regard to the roll-over bar, must pass between two parallel planes separated by 80cm.

Behind the front wheels, the coachwork shall not exceed a maximum width of 110cm.

This width does not include the crushable structure which will have a maximum width of 10cm each side. The overall width of the coachwork may thus extend to 130cm.

The coachwork ahead of the front wheels may be extended to an overall maximum width of 150cm.

Nevertheless, any part of the coachwork ahead of the front wheels, exceeding an overall width of 110cm, shall not extend above the height of the front wheel rims.

Art. 297. – Safety devices: the safety devices and measures given hereafter must be complied with for racing cars of the international formulae.

a) Roll-bars:

Dimensions: the dimensions of the roll-bars must be as follows: the minimum height must be at least 36in (92cm) measured along the line of the driver's spine, from the metal seat to the top of the roll-bar. The top of the roll-bar must also be at least 5cm above the driver's helmet, when the driver is sitting in normal driving position.

The width must be at least 38cm measured inside the roll-bar between the two vertical pillars of the sides. It must be measured at 60cm above the metal seat on the perpendicular to the line of the driver's spine.

Strength: in order to obtain a sufficient strength for the roll-bar, two possibilities are left to the manufacturers:

   a) The roll-over bar, of entirely free structural conception, must be capable to withstand the stress minima indicated under Art. 253 o) – III.

   b) The tubes and brace(s) must have a diameter of at least 1 $^3/_8$in (3.5cm) and at least 0.090in (2mm) wall thickness. The material should be molybdenum chromium SAE 4130 or SAE 4125 (or equivalent in DIN, NF, etc.).

There must be at least one brace from the top of the bar rearwards at an angle not exceeding 60° with the horizontal. The diameter and material of the brace must be the same as those of the roll-bar itself.

In the case of two braces, the diameter of each of them may be reduced to 20/26mm.

Removable connections between the main hoop and the brace must comply with drawings nos. 10 and 11 of Art. 253 or with any other type approved by the FIA.

b) Cables, lines and electrical equipment: except if the cables, lines and electrical equipment such as battery, fuel pump, etc., are in compliance with the requirements of the aircraft industry as regards their location, material and connections, they must be placed or fitted in such a way that any leakage cannot result in:

   – accumulation of liquid,
   – entry of liquid into the cockpit,
   – contact between liquid and any electrical line or equipment.

Should the cables, lines or electrical equipment pass through or be fitted in the cockpit, they must be fully enclosed in a cover of a liquid-tight and fire-proof material.

Petrol lines will be fitted with self-sealing breakaway couplings in compliance with the requirements of the aircraft industry as regards their location and material.

c) Safety fuel tanks

Refer to Article 293.

d) Red warning light:

All Formula cars must be equipped with a rearward-facing red warning light of at least 15 watts. This light must be mounted as high as possible on the centre-line of the car and be clearly visible from the rear. The warning light must be switched on by order of the clerk of the course.

e) Tank fillers and caps: it is recalled that on Formula cars, the tank fillers and their caps must not protrude beyond the coachwork.

The caps must be designed in such a way as to ensure an efficient locking action which reduces the risks of an accidental opening following a crash impact or incomplete locking after refuelling.

The fillers must be placed away from points which are vulnerable in case of a crash. The air vents must be located at least 25cm to the rear of the cockpit.

f) Electric circuit-breakers: it is recalled that since 1st January 1969, the fitting of a general electric circuit-breaker, clearly indicated, is mandatory for all cars taking part in speed races.

For Formula cars, this circuit-breaker must be indicated by a blue triangle with a spark and be easy to reach from inside as well as from outside the car.

g) Extinguishing system: All cars of the international racing formulae must be fitted with an extinguishing system conforming to Art. 269.

Art. 298. – Additional safety measures applicable to Formula 1.

a) At least half of the extinguishing capacity must be placed forward of the engine but rearward of the foremost pick-up points of the front suspension. Waivers to this rule may be given by the CSI for an installation which can be considered to be within the main structure of the car.

b) Provision for a clearly indicated external emergency handle which can be actuated easily by the circuit rescue personnel even at a distance with a hook. This emergency handle shall simultaneously initiate the fire-extinguisher, cut off the engine and isolate the battery.

c) Compulsory fitting of a headrest capable of restraining 17kg under a rearward acceleration of 9G. Its dimensions shall be such that in no case can the driver's head be trapped between the roll-over bar and the headrest itself.

d) The use of magnesium sheet will be authorized only if its thickness exceeds 3mm.

e) The battery must be capable of starting the engine at least twice. However, it will be possible to start the engine in the pits or on the dummy grid with an external power source. In that case, the starter socket must be installed at the rear of the car and must face rearwards. If male sockets are used, they must be recessed and be provided with a cover.

f) Chromium plating of steel suspension members of over 45 tons per sq in tensile strength is forbidden.

Art. 299. – Conditions required for international formula events.

Duration of FI Championship events:
The duration of FI Championship events shall be 200 miles or two hours, whichever is the shorter. Should two hours elapse before the scheduled race distance is completed, the leader will be shown the chequered flag at the end of the lap in which the period of two hours shall end.

Useful contacts

Adams McCall Engineering
The Workshop
Home Farm
Laverstoke Park
Nr Whitchurch
Hampshire RG28 7NT
Tel 01256 771666
■ *Historic racing car preparation.*

Avon Tyres Motorsport
Bath Road, Melksham
Wiltshire SN12 8AA
Tel 01225 703101
Website www.
avonmotorsport.com
■ *Tyre supplier for historic Formula 1 racing.*

Duncan Hamilton & Co.
PO Box 222, Hook
Nr Basingstoke
Hampshire RG27 9YZ
Tel 01256 765000
Website www.
duncanhamilton.com
■ *Classic and race car dealer.*

Ellis Clowes
27 Horse Fair, Banbury
Oxfordshire OX16 0AE
Tel 01295 221190
Website
www.ellisclowes.com
■ *Insurance broker.*

Geoff Richardson Racing Engines
7 Brook Road
Bicton Industrial Park
Kimbolton
Cambridgeshire PE28 0LR
Tel 01480 861599
Website www.
geoffrichardsonengines.
com
■ *Historic race engine supplier and rebuilder.*

Hagerty International
The Arch Barn
Pury Hill Farm
Towcester
Northamptonshire
NN12 7TB
Tel 0844 8241130
Website www.
hagertyinsurance.co.uk
■ *Insurance broker.*

Hall and Hall
Graham Hill Way
Cherry Holt Road
Bourne
Lincolnshire PE10 9PJ
Tel 01778 392562
Website
www.hallandhall.net
■ *Historic racing car sales, restoration and race preparation.*

Hewland Engineering
Waltham Road
White Waltham
Maidenhead
Berkshire SL6 3LR
Tel 01628 827600
Website
www.hewland.com
■ *Gearbox manufacturer.*

Historic Grand Prix
4 Finch Road
North Salem,
NY 10560, USA
Website www.
historicgrandprix.com
■ *Historic Formula 1 race organiser.*

Kumschick Racing
Luzernerstrasse 57
6247 Schötz
Luzern, Switzerland
Tel +41 41 980 05 08
Website www.
kumschickracing.ch
■ *Historic racing car preparation.*

Langford Performance Engineering
17 Bradfield Close
Finedon Road Industrial
Estate
Wellingborough NN8 4RQ
Tel 01933 441661
■ *New build and rebuild engines.*

Mandarin Motorsport
Unit 9 Flightway
Dunkeswell Business Park
Honiton
Devon EX14 4RD
Tel 01404 890084
■ *Historic racing car preparation.*

Masters Historic Racing
The Bunker
Lower End Road
Wavendon
Milton Keynes MK17 8DA
Tel 01908 587545
Website www.
themastersseries.com
■ *Organiser of the Grand Prix Masters series.*

Nicholson McLaren
12 Ivanhoe Road
Hogwood Lane
Finchampstead
Wokingham
Berkshire RG40 4QQ
Tel 0118 9738000
Website www.
nicholsonmclaren.com
■ *Engine build and preparation.*

Phil Reilly & Company
5842 Paradise Drive
Corte Madera
CA 94925, USA
Tel +1 (415) 924 9022
■ *Historic racing car preparation.*

R&J Simpson Engineering
Unit 3–4 Mariner
Lichfield Road Industrial
Estate, Tamworth
Staffordshire B79 7UL
Tel 01827 67898
Website
www.randjsimpson.com
■ *Restoration and reproduction of historic racing cars.*

Stuart McCrudden Associates
West Hall, Lea Lane
Great Braxted
Witham, Essex CM8 3EP
Tel 01621 892814
Website www.smapr.net
■ *Series and race organiser.*

WDK Motorsport Ltd
Unit 2
Houghton Down Farm
Salisbury Road
Stockbridge
Hampshire SO20 6JR
Tel 01264 811119
Website www.
wdkmotorsports.co.uk
■ *Historic racing car preparation.*

Wehrmann Engineering
70 Suffolk Ct Ste 500
Hauppauge
NY 11788-3759
Tel +1 (888) 598 9071
■ *Historic racing car preparation.*

Index